INSTRUCTOR'S RESOURCE MANUAL FOR

Issues & Ethics
IN THE
Helping Professions

SIXTH EDITION

Gerald Corey
California State University, Fullerton

Marianne Schneider Corey
Private Practice/Consultant

Patrick Callanan
Private Practice

BROOKS/COLE

THOMSON LEARNING

Australia • Canada • Mexico • Singapore • Spain • United Kingdom • United States

COPYRIGHT © 2003 Wadsworth Group.
Brooks/Cole is an imprint of the Wadsworth Group, a division of Thomson Learning, Inc.
Thomson Learning™ is a trademark used herein under license.

For more information about this or any other Brooks/Cole products, contact:
BROOKS/COLE
511 Forest Lodge Road
Pacific Grove, CA 93950 USA
www.brookscole.com
1-800-423-0563 (Thomson Learning Academic Resource Center)

Printed in the United States of America

10   9   8   7   6   5   4   3   2   1

ISBN: 0-534-51438-3

CONTENTS

PREFACE

We appreciate you adopting **Issues and Ethics in the Helping Professions, Sixth Edition**, and we sincerely hope that you and your students will find it a useful tool for promoting reflection and discussion on a range of cant issues. This manual offers some perspectives on teaching courses dealing with ethical and professional issues. The discussion focuses on assisting students in developing an ethical sense, the role of modeling of attitudes and behaviors on the part of the faculty, ways of teaching ethical decision making, surveys on the practices of teaching graduate courses in ethics, and trends in the teaching of ethics.

A sample course outline follows, with detailed writing assignments, schedule of topics and assignments for a semester course, and guidelines for students in getting the most from the course. The next section consists of a Study Guide for **Issues and Ethics in the Helping Professions, Sixth Edition**. There are some key questions to guide students in their reading and reviewing of each chapter. You may want to use some of these questions as catalysts for class discussion, for take-home written assignments, for small-group interaction, or for test questions. The questions highlight the core ideas of each chapter and also ask for student reaction to some topics. These questions can be included as part of the course syllabus as a way to focus students on key points for each chapter. The following section includes chapter quizzes for all thirteen chapters. These can be used to test the student weekly or combined to meet your criteria for testing. These questions were written to test the student's knowledge of the facts and concepts included in each chapter. There are also case study questions to test the student's ability to apply the knowledge learned through their readings and experiential exercises done in the classroom. There is a practice examination which is based on questions from the entire textbook. This practice examination is a useful tool for students to take at home prior to the final examination and to score as a comprehension check.

The next section is a final examination, which consists of **200** objective test items based on **Issues and Ethics in the Helping Professions, Sixth Edition**. In addition to the quizzes, practice examination items, and the final examination, there are also online quiz items available to students via the Internet, which are also reproduced in this manual. There are 10 questions for each of the 13 chapters for the online quizzes.

You will also find a listing of the InfoTrac key words (which are also listed at the end of each chapter in the textbook,) a list of professional organizations, website resources, a student evaluation of the course and the instructor, a listing of other books by the authors, and transparency masters for each chapter.

CD-ROM as a Supplement for Your Students. A new integrated learning package entitled **Ethics in Action CD-ROM** has been developed to enhance the sixth edition of Issues and Ethics in the Helping Professions. Ethics in Action CD-ROM is designed to bring to life the ethical issues and dilemmas that counselors often encounter and provide ample opportunity for discussion, self-exploration, and problem-solving of these issues and dilemmas – and can be used as supplementary exercises and activities for most of the chapters in the textbook. The video is based upon a weekend workshop co-led by Marianne Schneider Corey and Gerald Corey for a group of counseling students. The workshop included challenging questions and lively discussion, role-plays to bring the issues to life, and comments from the students and the Coreys. This supplementary learning tool, which is available at a reduced price to students if it is shrinkwrapped with the text, allows students to view role-plays dealing with common ethical dilemmas in a variety of settings, and gives them opportunities to review and expand their knowledge in a hands-on ways with interactive exercises and activities. After each role-play vignette in this CD-ROM, students are encouraged to take time to identify the issues in the role-play, examine their own values in the situation, and formulate a plan about how they would respond if they were the therapist in each of the situations depicted. This program is divided into three segments: ethical decision making, values and the helping relationship, and boundary issues and multiple relationships in counseling. At the end of Chapters 1 to 9 and 11 in the textbook, are suggested activities and guidelines for integrating the CD-ROM program with this textbook.

There is also an **Institutional Version of Ethics in Action**, along with a **Facilitator's Resource Manual**, structured around the same three topical areas as the **Ethics in Action CD-ROM**, but with different role-plays illustrating different ethical dilemmas. The **Institutional Version** is designed to be sold to colleges, universities, training programs, and community agencies that offer supervision of interns. The **Ethics in Action: Institutional Video** is directly linked to Chapters 1, 2, 3, 4, and 7 of **Issues and Ethics in the Helping Professions, Sixth Edition**. This video is available for department purchase through Thomson Learning Customer Service. To receive a Preview Video and Workbook, please use ISBN 0-534-57638-9. Complimentary **Facilitator's Resource Guide** is also available to purchasers of the video: 0-534-35621-4.

Another valuable tool for your students is the new, inexpensive booklet, **Codes of Ethics for the Helping Professions**, which offers codes of ethics for the major helping professional organizations such as APA, ACA, NASW, NOHSE, ASCA, AAMFT, and others. The advantage of this booklet is that students can have the complete code of ethics of the professional organizations in one place for frequent reference. This booklet, **Codes of Ethics for the Helping Professions**, can be a part of the integrated learning package as a shrink wrap option with the textbook.

For other supplementary tools available to you, see the Preface of the Instructor's Edition of Issues and Ethics and also see the Resource Integration Guide, which follows this preface in this Instructor's Resource Manual.

We would like to acknowledge our thanks to Laura Donahue for proofreading and getting this IRM into camera ready copy; to Shelley Gesicki, project editor who supported our efforts; Mary Lou O'Phelan of Century College for her work on the original transparency masters; to John Perry for his work on the Resource Integration Guide, the revision of the transparency masters, and doing a search for the InfoTrac key words.

Chapter 1 Introduction to Professional Ethics

Ideas for Instruction	Media Resources for Instructors	Media Resources for Students
Instructor's Resource Manual: Part 1 — Perspectives on the Teaching of Ethics Part 2 — Course Outline for Ethical and Professional Issues	**Web Site** (web icon): http://counseling.wadsworth.com/corey/index.html Access many online resources for you and your students.	**Web Site** (web icon): http://counseling.wadsworth.com/corey/index.html For InfoTrac keywords, online quiz items, weblinks to professional organizations and other resources.
Instructor's Resource Manual: Part 3 — Focus questions for discussion and reflection (Ch. 1) Part 4 — Chapter Quiz Part 7 — Online Quiz Items (Ch. 1) Part 9 — InfoTrac Key Words	Ethics in Action: Institutional Version: **Available only for instructional purposes, the institutional features role-plays and discussions not f the student CD-ROM. See segment 1 "F Me".**	**Ethics in Action: CD-ROM** A unique multimedia learning tool that allows students to view role-plays dealing with common ethical dilemmas, and gives them the opportunity to review and expand their knowledge with interactive exercises and activities.
Instructor's Resource Manual: Part 5 — Practice Comprehensive Exam Part 6 — Final Comprehensive Exam Part 10 — Professional Organizations and Web Site Resources	**PowerPoint:** Slides available for download at the web site http://counseling.wadsworth.com/corey/index.html	**InfoTrac College Edition** (logo) **Keywords:** See "Issues and Ethics" page 33.
"Issues and Ethics" text: Suggested Activities pp. 30–32. Internet Resources pp. 31–32	**Transparency Masters:** Transparencies 2–6. See part 13 of this Resource Manual.	**Ethics Codes for the Helping Professions:** This compact, inexpensive resource offers the codes of ethics for the major helping professional organizations.
	ExamView® Test Wizard: Create tests based on Issues & Ethics.	

Chapter 2 The Counselor as a Person and as a Professional

Ideas for Instruction	Media Resources for Instructors	Media Resources for Students
Instructor's Resource Manual: Part 3 — Focus questions for discussion and reflection (Ch. 2) Part 4 — Chapter Quiz Part 7 — Online Quiz Items (Ch. 2) Part 9 — InfoTrac Key Words	**Web Site** (web icon): http://counseling.wadsworth.com/corey/index.html Access many online resources for you and your students.	**Web Site** (web icon): http://counseling.wadsworth.com/corey/index.html For InfoTrac keywords, online quiz items, weblinks to professional organizations and other resources.
Instructor's Resource Manual: Part 5 — Practice Comprehensive Exam Part 6 — Final Comprehensive Exam Part 10 — Professional Organizations and Web Site Resources	Ethics in Action: Institutional Version: **Available only for instructional purposes, the institutional features role-plays and discussions not f the student CD-ROM. See segment 1 "R Kids".**	**Ethics in Action: CD-ROM** A multimedia learning tool that provides role-plays dealing with common ethical dilemmas, exercises and activities. See role play #2 "Big Brother".
"Issues and Ethics" text: Pre-Chapter Self-Inventory pp. 34–35. Suggested Activities pp. 68–69.	**PowerPoint:** Slides available for download at the web site http://counseling.wadsworth.com/corey/index.html	**InfoTrac College Edition** (logo) **Keywords:** See "Issues and Ethics" page 69.
	Transparency Masters: Transparencies 7–12. See part 13 of this Resource Manual.	
	ExamView® Test Wizard: Create tests based on Issues & Ethics.	

Chapter 3 Values and the Helping Relationship

Ideas for Instruction	Media Resources for Instructors	Media Resources for Students
Instructor's Resource Manual: Part 3 — Focus questions for discussion and reflection (Ch. 3) Part 4 — Chapter Quiz Part 7 — Online Quiz Items (Ch. 3) Part 9 — InfoTrac Key Words	**Web Site** (web icon): http://counseling.wadsworth.com/corey/index.html Access many online resources for you and your students.	**Web Site** (web icon): http://counseling.wadsworth.com/corey/index.html For InfoTrac keywords, online quiz items, weblinks to professional organizations and other resources.
Instructor's Resource Manual: Part 5 — Practice Comprehensive Exam Part 6 — Final Comprehensive Exam Part 10 — Professional Organizations and Web Site Resources	Ethics in Action: **Institutional Version:** Available only for instructional purposes, the institutional version features role-plays and discussions not found on the student CD-ROM. See segment 2 "Religion as Answer", "Abortion", "Coming Out", and "End-of-Life Decisions".	**Ethics in Action: CD-ROM** A unique multimedia learning tool that allows students to view role-plays dealing with common ethical dilemmas, and gives them the opportunity to review and expand their knowledge with interactive exercises and activities. See role plays #4 "The Divorce", #5 "Doing It My Way", and #6 "The Promiscuous One".
"Issues and Ethics" text: Pre-Chapter Self-Inventory pp. 70–71. Suggested Activities pp. 104–106.	**PowerPoint:** Slides available for download at the web site http://counseling.wadsworth.com/corey/index.html	**InfoTrac College Edition** (logo) **Keywords:** See "Issues and Ethics" page 107.
	Transparency Masters: Transparencies 13–18. See part 13 of this Resource Manual.	
	ExamView® Test Wizard: Create tests based on Issues & Ethics.	

Chapter 4 Multicultural Perspectives and Diversity Issues

Ideas for Instruction	Media Resources for Instructors	Media Resources for Students
Instructor's Resource Manual: Part 3 — Focus questions for discussion and reflection (Ch. 4) Part 4 — Chapter Quiz Part 7 — Online Quiz Items (Ch. 4) Part 9 — InfoTrac Key Words	**Web Site** (web icon): http://counseling.wadsworth.com/corey/index.html Access many online resources for you and your students.	**Web Site** (web icon): http://counseling.wadsworth.com/corey/index.html For InfoTrac keywords, online quiz items, weblinks to professional organizations and other resources.
Instructor's Resource Manual: Part 5 — Practice Comprehensive Exam Part 6 — Final Comprehensive Exam Part 10 — Professional Organizations and Web Site Resources	Ethics in Action: **Institutional Version:** Available only for instructional purposes, the institutional version features role-plays and discussions not found on the student CD-ROM. See segment 1 "Seeking More from Life", and segment 2 "Coming Out".	**Ethics in Action: CD-ROM** A unique multimedia learning tool that allows students to view role-plays dealing with common ethical dilemmas, and gives them the opportunity to review and expand their knowledge with interactive exercises and activities. See role play #3 "Culture Clash".
"Issues and Ethics" text: Pre-Chapter Self-Inventory pp. 108–109. Suggested Activities pp. 142–144.	**PowerPoint:** Slides available for download at the web site http://counseling.wadsworth.com/corey/index.html	**InfoTrac College Edition** (logo) **Keywords:** See "Issues and Ethics" page 145.
	Transparency Masters: Transparencies 19–30. See part 13 of this Resource Manual.	
	ExamView® Test Wizard: Create tests based on Issues & Ethics.	

Chapter 5 Client Rights and Counselor Responsibilities

Ideas for Instruction	Media Resources for Instructors	Media Resources for Students
Instructor's Resource Manual: Part 3 — Focus questions for discussion and reflection (Ch. 5) Part 4 — Chapter Quiz Part 7 — Online Quiz Items (Ch. 5) Part 9 — InfoTrac Key Words	**Web Site** (web icon): http://counseling.wadsworth.com/corey/index.html Access many online resources for you and your students.	**Web Site** (web icon): http://counseling.wadsworth.com/corey index.html For InfoTrac keywords, online quiz items, weblinks to professional organizations and other resources.
Instructor's Resource Manual: Part 5 — Practice Comprehensive Exam Part 6 — Final Comprehensive Exam Part 10 — Professional Organizations and Web Site Resources	**PowerPoint:** Slides available for download at the web site http://counseling.wadsworth.com/corey/index.html	**Ethics in Action: CD-ROM** A unique multimedia learning tool that allows students to view role-plays dealing with common ethical dilemmas, and gives them the opportunity to review and expand their knowledge with interactive exercises and activities. See role play #7 "The Affair", #4 "The Divorce", & #1 "Teen Pregnancy".
"Issues and Ethics" text: Pre-Chapter Self-Inventory pp. 146–147. Suggested Activities pp. 191–193.	**Transparency Masters:** Transparencies 31–38. See part 13 of this Resource Manual.	**InfoTrac College Edition** (logo) **Keywords:** See "Issues and Ethics" page 193.
	ExamView® Test Wizard: Create tests based on Issues & Ethics.	

Chapter 6 Confidentiality: Ethical and Legal Issues

Ideas for Instruction	Media Resources for Instructors	Media Resources for Students
Instructor's Resource Manual: Part 3 — Focus questions for discussion and reflection (Ch. 6) Part 4 — Chapter Quiz Part 7 — Online Quiz Items (Ch. 6) Part 9 — InfoTrac Key Words	**Web Site** (web icon): http://counseling.wadsworth.com/corey/index.html Access many online resources for you and your students.	**Web Site** (web icon): http://counseling.wadsworth.com/corey index.html For InfoTrac keywords, online quiz items, weblinks to professional organizations and other resources.
Instructor's Resource Manual: Part 5 — Practice Comprehensive Exam Part 6 — Final Comprehensive Exam Part 10 — Professional Organizations and Web Site Resources	**PowerPoint:** Slides available for download at the web site http://counseling.wadsworth.com/corey/index.html	**Ethics in Action: CD-ROM** A unique multimedia learning tool that allows students to view role-plays dealing with common ethical dilemmas, and gives them the opportunity to review and expand their knowledge with interactive exercises and activities. See role play #6 "The Promiscuous One".
"Issues and Ethics" text: Pre-Chapter Self-Inventory pp. 194–195. Suggested Activities pp. 242–243.	**Transparency Masters:** Transparencies 39–47. See part 13 of this Resource Manual.	**InfoTrac College Edition** (logo) **Keywords:** See "Issues and Ethics" page 243.
	ExamView® Test Wizard: Create tests based on Issues & Ethics.	

Chapter 7 Managing Boundaries and Multiple Relationships

Ideas for Instruction	Media Resources for Instructors	Media Resources for Students
Instructor's Resource Manual: Part 3 — Focus questions for discussion and reflection (Ch. 7) Part 4 — Chapter Quiz Part 7 — Online Quiz Items (Ch. 7) Part 9 — InfoTrac Key Words	**Web Site** (web icon): http://counseling.wadsworth.com/corey/index.html Access many online resources for you and your students.	**Web Site** (web icon): http://counseling.wadsworth.com/corey/index.html For InfoTrac keywords, online quiz items, weblinks to professional organizations and other resources.
Instructor's Resource Manual: Part 5 — Practice Comprehensive Exam Part 6 — Final Comprehensive Exam Part 10 — Professional Organizations and Web Site Resources	Ethics in Action: **Institutional Version:** Available only for instructional purposes, the institutional version features role-plays and discussions not found on the student CD-ROM. See segment 3 "The Wedding", "Client's Attraction", "Manacuring for Therapy", and "The Vase".	**Ethics in Action: CD-ROM** A multimedia learning tool that provides role-plays dealing with common ethical dilemmas, exercises and activities. See role play #8 "The Picnic", #9 "The Friendship", #10 "The Disclosure", #11 "The Architect", #12 "Tickets for Therapy".
"Issues and Ethics" text: Pre-Chapter Self-Inventory pp. 244–245. Suggested Activities pp. 289–291.	**PowerPoint:** Slides available for download at the web site http://counseling.wadsworth.com/corey/index.html	**InfoTrac College Edition** (logo) **Keywords:** See "Issues and Ethics" page 291.
	Transparency Masters: Transparencies 48–55. See part 13 of this Resource Manual.	
	ExamView® Test Wizard: Create tests based on Issues & Ethics.	

Chapter 8 Professional Competence and Training

Ideas for Instruction	Media Resources for Instructors	Media Resources for Students
Instructor's Resource Manual: Part 3 — Focus questions for discussion and reflection (Ch. 8) Part 4 — Chapter Quiz Part 7 — Online Quiz Items (Ch. 8) Part 9 — InfoTrac Key Words	**Web Site** (web icon): http://counseling.wadsworth.com/corey/index.html Access many online resources for you and your students.	**Web Site** (web icon): http://counseling.wadsworth.com/corey/index.html For InfoTrac keywords, online quiz items, weblinks to professional organizations and other resources.
Instructor's Resource Manual: Part 5 — Practice Comprehensive Exam Part 6 — Final Comprehensive Exam Part 10 — Professional Organizations and Web Site Resources	**PowerPoint:** Slides available for download at the web site http://counseling.wadsworth.com/corey/index.html	**Ethics in Action: CD-ROM** A unique multimedia learning tool that allows students to view role-plays dealing with common ethical dilemmas, and gives them the opportunity to review and expand their knowledge with interactive exercises and activities. Reflect on all role-plays.
"Issues and Ethics" text: Pre-Chapter Self-Inventory pp. 292–293. Suggested Activities pp. 315–317.	**Transparency Masters:** Transparencies 56–59. See part 13 of this Resource Manual.	**InfoTrac College Edition** (logo) **Keywords:** See "Issues and Ethics" page 317.
	ExamView® Test Wizard: Create tests based on Issues & Ethics.	

Chapter 9 Issues in Supervision and Consultation

Ideas for Instruction	Media Resources for Instructors	Media Resources for Students
Instructor's Resource Manual: Part 3 — Focus questions for discussion and reflection (Ch. 9) Part 4 — Chapter Quiz Part 7 — Online Quiz Items (Ch. 9) Part 9 — InfoTrac Key Words	**Web Site** (web icon): http://counseling.wadsworth.com/corey/ index.html Access many online resources for you and your students.	**Web Site** (web icon): http://counseling.wadsworth.com/corey index.html For InfoTrac keywords, online quiz items, weblinks to professional organizations and other resources.
Instructor's Resource Manual: Part 5 — Practice Comprehensive Exam Part 6 — Final Comprehensive Exam Part 10 — Professional Organizations and Web Site Resources	**PowerPoint:** Slides available for download at the web site http://counseling.wadsworth.com/corey/ index.html	**Ethics in Action: CD-ROM** A unique multimedia learning tool that allows students to view role-plays dealing with common ethical dilemmas, and gives them the opportunity to review and expand their knowledge with interactive exercises and activities. Reflect on all role-plays.
"Issues and Ethics" text: Pre-Chapter Self-Inventory pp. 318–319. Suggested Activities pp. 351–353.	**Transparency Masters:** Transparencies 60–64. See part 13 of this Resource Manual.	**InfoTrac College Edition** (logo) **Keywords:** See "Issues and Ethics" page 353.
	ExamView® Test Wizard: Create tests based on Issues & Ethics.	

Chapter 10 Issues in Theory, Practice, and Research

Ideas for Instruction	Media Resources for Instructors	Media Resources for Students
Instructor's Resource Manual: Part 3 — Focus questions for discussion and reflection (Ch. 10) Part 4 — Chapter Quiz Part 7 — Online Quiz Items (Ch. 10) Part 9 — InfoTrac Key Words	**Web Site** (web icon): http://counseling.wadsworth.com/corey/ index.html Access many online resources for you and your students.	**Web Site** (web icon): http://counseling.wadsworth.com/corey index.html For InfoTrac keywords, online quiz items, weblinks to professional organizations and other resources.
Instructor's Resource Manual: Part 5 — Practice Comprehensive Exam Part 6 — Final Comprehensive Exam Part 10 — Professional Organizations and Web Site Resources	**PowerPoint:** Slides available for download at the web site http://counseling.wadsworth.com/corey/ index.html	**InfoTrac College Edition** (logo) **Keywords:** See "Issues and Ethics" page 393.
"Issues and Ethics" text: Pre-Chapter Self-Inventory pp. 354–355. Suggested Activities pp. 391–393.	**Transparency Masters:** Transparencies 65–72. See part 13 of this Resource Manual.	
	ExamView® Test Wizard: Create tests based on Issues & Ethics.	

Chapter 11 Ethical Issues in Couples and Family Therapy

Ideas for Instruction	Media Resources for Instructors	Media Resources for Students
Instructor's Resource Manual: Part 3 — Focus questions for discussion and reflection (Ch. 11) Part 4 — Chapter Quiz Part 7 — Online Quiz Items (Ch. 11) Part 9 — InfoTrac Key Words	**Web Site** (web icon): http://counseling.wadsworth.com/corey/index.html Access many online resources for you and your students.	**Web Site** (web icon): http://counseling.wadsworth.com/corey/index.html For InfoTrac keywords, online quiz items, weblinks to professional organizations and other resources.
Instructor's Resource Manual: Part 5 — Practice Comprehensive Exam Part 6 — Final Comprehensive Exam Part 10 — Professional Organizations and Web Site Resources	**PowerPoint:** Slides available for download at the web site http://counseling.wadsworth.com/corey/index.html	**Ethics in Action: CD-ROM** A unique multimedia learning tool that allows students to view role-plays dealing with common ethical dilemmas, and gives them the opportunity to review and expand their knowledge with interactive exercises and activities. See role play #4 "The Divorce".
"Issues and Ethics" text: Pre-Chapter Self-Inventory pp. 394–395. Suggested Activities pp. 417–418.	**Transparency Masters:** Transparencies 73–77. See part 13 of this Resource Manual.	**InfoTrac College Edition** (logo) **Keywords:** See "Issues and Ethics" page 418.
	ExamView® Test Wizard: Create tests based on Issues & Ethics.	

Chapter 12 Ethical Issues in Group Work

Ideas for Instruction	Media Resources for Instructors	Media Resources for Students
Instructor's Resource Manual: Part 3 — Focus questions for discussion and reflection (Ch. 12) Part 4 — Chapter Quiz Part 7 — Online Quiz Items (Ch. 12) Part 9 — InfoTrac Key Words	**Web Site** (web icon): http://counseling.wadsworth.com/corey/index.html Access many online resources for you and your students.	**Web Site** (web icon): http://counseling.wadsworth.com/corey/index.html For InfoTrac keywords, online quiz items, weblinks to professional organizations and other resources.
Instructor's Resource Manual: Part 5 — Practice Comprehensive Exam Part 6 — Final Comprehensive Exam Part 10 — Professional Organizations and Web Site Resources	**PowerPoint:** Slides available for download at the web site http://counseling.wadsworth.com/corey/index.html	**InfoTrac College Edition** (logo) **Keywords:** See "Issues and Ethics" page 443.
"Issues and Ethics" text: Pre-Chapter Self-Inventory pp. 420–421. Suggested Activities pp. 442–443.	**Transparency Masters:** Transparencies 78–82. See part 13 of this Resource Manual.	
	ExamView® Test Wizard: Create tests based on Issues & Ethics.	

Chapter 13 Ethical Issues in Community Work

Ideas for Instruction	Media Resources for Instructors	Media Resources for Students
Instructor's Resource Manual: Part 3 — Focus questions for discussion and reflection (Ch. 13) Part 4 — Chapter Quiz Part 7 — Online Quiz Items (Ch. 13) Part 9 — InfoTrac Key Words	**Web Site** (web icon): http://counseling.wadsworth.com/corey/index.html Access many online resources for you and your students.	**Web Site** (web icon): http://counseling.wadsworth.com/corey/index.html For InfoTrac keywords, online quiz items, weblinks to professional organizations and other resources.
Instructor's Resource Manual: Part 5 — Practice Comprehensive Exam Part 6 — Final Comprehensive Exam Part 10 — Professional Organizations and Web Site Resources	**PowerPoint:** Slides available for download at the web site http://counseling.wadsworth.com/corey/index.html	**InfoTrac College Edition** (logo) **Keywords:** See "Issues and Ethics" page 472–473.
"Issues and Ethics" text: Pre-Chapter Self-Inventory pp. 444–445. Suggested Activities pp. 471–472.	**Transparency Masters:** Transparencies 83–87. See part 13 of this Resource Manual.	
	ExamView® Test Wizard: Create tests based on Issues & Ethics.	

PART 1

PERSPECTIVES ON THE TEACHING OF ETHICS

What follows is some material that we hope instructors will find useful in designing an ethics course and in developing a course outline. Some of the following material can be included in a course outline or in a handout that is given to students at the beginning of the course. We focus on the role of faculty modeling and also explore some of the goals of teaching ethics. Since there are different approaches to presenting an ethics course, we summarize some perspectives on the teaching of ethics, and highlight some trends in the field.

The Formation of an Ethical Sense

For students, developing an ethical sense includes committing themselves to their education, being an active learner, learning from role models such as their professors, and getting involved in related course work. From our perspective the cultivation of an ethical sense begins with students commitment to their education in the helping professions. The way they approach their education has a bearing on the way they will approach their professional career. If they are committed to their studies on both an intellectual and emotional level, they will probably bring this enthusiasm and dedication to their professional practice. Of course, there are those students who are committed to manipulating the system so that they can merely get by with minimal effort. Some take the shortest route to earning a degree and getting a license, and once they attain these goals, they stop learning. We are convinced that these people are limited in their capacity to help others.

In addition to being active learners, it is essential, we think, that students be aware of their motivations for choosing the helping professions as a career. The motivations for being a helper are related to the development of an ethical sense. Although many personal needs can be met through helping others, it is crucial that these needs not be met at the expense of the client. Those who make a lifetime commitment to helping others have a responsibility to be clear about what they are getting from their work and how their personal characteristics play a vital role in their ability to make appropriate ethical decisions. Note: The bibliographic references indicated in the sections below can be found in the References at the end of this section.

Role of Faculty Modeling in Teaching Students Ethics

We contend that the faculty of any program in the helping professions plays a major role in modeling an ethical sense. The ways in which the faculty members teach their courses and relate to and supervise students have a significant impact. For example, supervisors may model confidentiality or the lack of it by how they talk about their own clients. As Kitchener (1984) has pointed out, one way of teaching students what it means to be an ethical professional is by being truthful, honest, and direct with them. The faculty members must be open to honest self-exploration of the ethical issues they face if they hope to have an impact on their students ability to think from an ethical perspective. Kitchener (1986) puts this matter well: By modeling, through discussions, and by valuing ethical behavior, counselor educators can encourage young professionals to develop a sense of responsibility to act in an ethically responsible manner. Also, they can help them learn to tolerate the ambiguity involved in ethical decision making. First, however, counselor educators must learn to tolerate ambiguity themselves [1986, p. 310].

We agree with the contention of Engels, Wilborn, and Schneider (1990) concerning the importance of professors and supervisors taking the risks involved in good learning and good counseling practice. They see it as imperative that faculty members engage in ongoing self-examination regarding personal and professional values, ethics, competence, and dedication. They emphasize that the best route to teaching these characteristics is by their modeling. Our students are likely to be more influenced by what we are actually doing than by what we say others should be doing. According to Tabachnick, Keith-Spiegel, and Pope (1991), there has been a lack of comprehensive and systematic data concerning the beliefs and behaviors of psychologists who function as educators. Their study was based on the assumption that there is a need to research which aspects of teaching are viewed as presenting ethical dilemmas for psychologists, how often those dilemmas occur, and how psychologists respond to the ethical issues they face as educators. Survey data were collected from psychologists who worked in higher education. They were asked the degree to which they engaged in 63 behaviors and the degree to which they considered each of these to be ethical. Of these 63 behaviors, 6 were very difficult for participants to evaluate on the basis of ethics, and 10 were exceptionally controversial. Based on the outcomes of their survey, Tabachnick et al. concluded that psychologists who serve as educators could benefit by a process of ethical self-examination and accountability. They encouraged psychologists to model through their teaching the self-reflection on ethical issues that they expect of their students. The authors stated, A crucial aspect of the maturation and moral development of any profession is the collective openness and dedication of its membership to study and critically examine itself (p. 515). They suggest that it is time for psychologists to bring the strategies and rigorous discipline of psychology to their own behavior and beliefs as teachers.

Ways of Teaching Ethical Decision Making

Kitchener (1986) has suggested that ethics training should create sensitivity to the ethical issues in the profession and to the implications of professional actions; should improve the ability to reason about ethical issues; should instill the determination to act in ethical ways; and should teach tolerance of ambiguity in ethical decision making as opposed to rigid indoctrination of right and wrong.

We endorse the practice of teaching students the process of making ethical decisions from the very beginning of their training program. The teaching of ethics can be conceptualized as progressing from a focus on theoretical issues to a stress on practical issues. When students are introduced to ethics education, it is likely that the emphasis will be on teaching general principles of ethical reasoning. Specific application can involve creating situations in the classroom in which students are challenged to apply ethical principles to specific cases.

Our Approach to the Teaching of Ethics

Two of us (Patrick Callanan and Gerald Corey) regularly co-teach an ethics course for undergraduate students in the Human Services Department at California State University, Fullerton. Rather than rely on lecture methods, we do our best to involve our students in identifying and examining the basic ethical principles involved in a variety of ethical dilemmas. Toward the goal of increasing student involvement, we do a good deal of role playing and dramatizing vignettes. Frequently, we assume the role of devil's advocate and challenge students to come up with reasons for whatever position they might assume. We ask our students to bring their concerns about the issues in the assigned readings. As much as possible, we attempt to facilitate interaction and discussion within the classroom. Our hope is that students will develop an appreciation for the value of thinking through ethical dilemmas by examining their own motivations and values. We ask students to be alert to the subtle ways that they might be ethically insensitive at times. We consistently encourage them to focus on their own motivations and behavior, rather than developing a judgmental stance by critiquing the ethics of others. Although many of our students do not have much practical experience in the field, we typically bring in practical examples and dilemmas that we expect they may eventually encounter. Through feedback from our students, we typically find case vignettes to be an effective way of developing decision-making attitudes and skills.

Teaching at the Graduate Level

Graduate courses in ethics at both the beginning and the end of the program are an ideal way to provide students with opportunities to grapple with ethical principles and apply them to practice. What are some practices in the teaching of ethics? A national survey of 289 master s programs in psychology assessed the type of ethics training that was available (Handelsman, 1986a). The results of this survey indicated that 87% of these programs had some format for teaching ethics; 29% had a formal and separate course in ethics; 47% taught ethics as a part of a formal course; and 11% dealt with ethical issues in informal ways through discussion during practicum and internship supervision sessions. Although 98.5% of the respondents believed that ethics could be taught adequately at the master's level, only 57% of them would recommend a formal course devoted entirely to ethics. Handelsman concluded that ethical thinking should be regarded as a skill, which can and ought to be taught in formal courses. Engels, Wilborn, and Schneider (1990) believe that ethics education is best taught in an ongoing way and that ethics can be infused in every aspect of the program. They favor including a didactic course in ethics and professional issues as a means of pulling together threads from many diverse aspects of training and for presenting aggregate information in a systematic and formal way. Lipsitz (1985) reports that the literature reveals a sevenfold increase in the availability of training experiences over the last 30 years. It appears that both formal and integrated ethics training are well respected by students who have been exposed to them. Ninety-two percent of the participants in the Lipsitz study were exposed to some systematic attempt to incorporate the topic of professional ethics into their curriculum. Of this group, 51% had a formal course in ethics, and 41% received ethics training that was integrated throughout their program.

Handelsman (1986b) presents a persuasive case for reconceptualizing ethics education. Contending that there are problems with ethics training by osmosis, he maintains that ethical thinking is a skill that must be developed through formal courses devoted primarily to ethics. For him, relying exclusively on informal methods alone, such as teaching ethics in the context of supervision, is a dangerous practice.

As Welfel and Lipsitz (1984) point out, however, more research is needed to determine the impact of formal course work in ethics. These authors contend that the literature only very weakly supports the interpretation that ethics courses have a positive impact on students. There is no study dealing with the influence of ethics training on actual behavior with clients. There are also no data to determine whether ethics is better taught in a separate course or integrated into existing courses in the curriculum. Welfel and Lipsitz raise the question of whether knowing ethical codes and learning a way of thinking and dealing with ethical dilemmas will actually be translated into actual practice. They acknowledge that progress has been made over the last 30 years in ethics education, but they ask if this increased attention to ethics training says much about the quality of this training. They assert that ethics courses are likely to fall short of their ultimate goals despite the best intentions of those who teach them.

Trends in the Teaching of Ethics

The process of learning to become an ethical practitioner begins with counselor-education programs, which normally include seminars in ethical principles and practices. Students should, as a beginning, thoroughly familiarize themselves with established ethical standards. They need to be sensitive to any ethical problems that arise in their practicum experiences and then discuss the problems in a seminar session or consult their supervisor. Part of a counselor's training is developing a sense of sound judgment, and dealing with basic ethical issues can assist in that development. Fortunately, there is a clear trend toward introducing counselors-in- training to the kinds of ethical and legal issues that they are likely to encounter. In reviewing the state of ethical training for counseling psychology doctoral students, Wilson and Ranft (1993) concluded that ethics training in graduate psychology programs has blossomed in the last decade. The results of their survey indicated that 94% of counseling psychology programs require training in ethics. Students in these programs feel prepared for both ethical and legal issues that are likely to arise in their professional roles. They claim that they feel more prepared in the decision-making process than in factual information of ethics.

The increased interest given to ethics education is related to an increase in malpractice litigation. The greater consciousness in the human-services professions about ethical and legal responsibilities parallels a concurrent rise in public consciousness about legal rights. There is a great deal of professional concern over identifying appropriate actions in the face of conflicting ethical, legal, and professional demands (Haas, Malouf, & Mayerson, 1986). Most of the attention has been given to violations of confidentiality and to sexual intimacies with clients. Other types of unethical behaviors have been documented, however, such as misrepresentation of skills, problems in the methods of collecting fees, improper use of assessment techniques, faulty diagnosis, treatment error, failure to respect client integrity, inappropriate public statements, violation of civil rights, assault and battery, and unethical research practices (Lipsitz, 1985; Pope, 1986). A trend that we would like to see in the teaching of ethics is for educators to demonstrate a willingness to engage in open discussion with their students about their own ethical beliefs. We would also hope that educators would realize the value of teaching ethical behavior through the process of modeling ethical practices by the way they relate to students in their classes.

It is our view that formal course work in ethics, both in separate courses and through an integrated approach with the rest of the curriculum, will significantly help students benefit from supervised fieldwork. The course work can alert students to ethical, legal, and professional issues that they might not have looked for, and they will be able to bring to their fieldwork questions about the ethical dimensions of their practice.

References

Engels, D., Wilborn, B. L., & Schneider, L. J. (1990). Ethics curricula for counselor preparation programs. In B. Herlihy, & L. B. Golden (Eds.), AACD ethical standards casebook (4th ed.) (pp. 111 126). Alexandria, VA: American Association for Counseling and Development.

Haas, L. J., Malouf, J. L., & Mayerson, N. H. (1986). Ethical dilemmas in psychological practice: Results of a national survey. Professional Psychology: Research and Practice, 17(4), 316 - 321.

Handelsman, M. M. (1986a). Ethics training at the master's level: A national survey. Professional Psychology: Research and Practice, 17(1), 24 - 26.

Handelsman, M. M. (1986b). Problems with ethics training by osmosis. Professional Psychology: Research and Practice, 17(4), 371 - 372.

Kitchener, K. S. (1984). Intuition, critical evaluation and ethical principles: The foundation for ethical decisions in counseling psychology. The Counseling Psychologist, 12(3), 43 - 55.

Kitchener, K. S. (1986). Teaching applied ethics in counselor education: An integration of psychological processes and philosophical analysis. Journal of Counseling and Development, 64(5), 306 - 310.

Lipsitz, N. E. (1985). The relationship between ethics training and ethical discrimination ability. Paper presented at the annual meeting of the American Psychological Association, Los Angeles.

Pope, K. S. (1986). New trends in malpractice cases and changes in APA's liability insurance. Independent Practitioner, 6(4), 23 - 26.

Tabachnick, B. G., Keith-Spiegel, P., & Pope, K. S. (1991). Ethics of teaching: Beliefs and behaviors of psychologists as educators. American Psychologist, 46(5), 506 - 515.

Weifel, E. R., & Lipsitz, N. E. (1984). The ethical behavior of professional psychologists: A critical analysis of the research. The Counseling Psychologist, 12(3), 31 - 42.

Wilson, L. S., & Ranft, V. A. (1993). The state of ethical training for counseling psychology doctoral students. The Counseling Psychologist, 21(3), 445 - 456.

PART 2

COURSE OUTLINE

HUSR 400
ETHICAL AND PROFESSIONAL ISSUES IN HUMAN SERVICES
[3 Semester Units]
FALL 2002—WEDNESDAYS from 4:00 to 6:45

Dr. Jerry Corey, Human Services Department
Office Hours: 3:00-4:00 on Wednesday. Human Services Office phone is 278-2255. Home phone is (909) 659-4320.

Basic Readings for HUSR 400 (Required)
Required Readings for HUSR 400:

1. Corey, G., Corey, M., and Callanan, P. (2003). **Issues and Ethics in the Helping Professions** (6th ed.). Pacific Grove, CA: Brooks/Cole.

2. **Ethics in Action CD-ROM** is packaged with Issues and Ethics text at a discount. It is required that you complete all the exercises and activities in this CD-ROM program. There is also an institutional version of the **Ethics in Action** video, which will be shown in class.

3. Also packaged with the text is a booklet containing the codes of the major professional organizations, **Ethics Codes for the Helping Professions,** which will be of use to you during the entire course.

Objectives of the Course: To stimulate you to think about major issues related to professional practice in human services and to challenge you to formulate a position on issues. To familiarize you with the ethics codes and to develop an ability to apply these codes to a variety of specific problem situations.

SCHEDULE FOR READINGS AND ASSIGNMENTS FOR FALL 2002

WEEKS		**TOPICS FOR DISCUSSION AND ASSIGNED READINGS**
(1)	August 21 Week 1	**Introduction to Course** **Introduction to Professional Ethics** **Chapter 1 -- Self-Inventory** (Discuss in class) **Videos: Ethics in Action: Institutional Version (Part I)** and **Video: ACA Video:** Part on Introduction to Ethics
(2)	August 28 Week 2	**Ethical Models and Ethical Decision Making Process** **Foundations of Ethical Practice: Basic Concepts** Complete Reading due of Chapter 1 and also CD-ROM program (Part I) **CD-ROM Program: Part I (Ethics in Action: Ethical Decision Making, and complete the activities.)** *Take-Home Quiz #1 on Chapter 1 due on August 28

*For each QUIZ, use the answer form. In addition to the QUIZ, which you are to score, complete the Pre-Chapter Self-Inventory at the beginning of each chapter in **Issues and Ethics** and put your responses on the answer form also. Along with Quiz #1 write your responses to the **Self-Assessment** (on pages 22 to 30 in Chapter 1).

| (3) | September 4
Week 3 | **Chapter 2 The Counselor as a Person and as a Professional**
Also --- **Introduction to Values**
Take-Home Quiz #2 on Chapter 2 due September 4
Videos: Ethics in Action: Institutional Video (Part II) |

(4)	September 11 Week 4	**Chapter 3 Values and the Helping Relationship** **Role of Values in Counseling Practice** **Take-Home Quiz #3 on Chapter 3 due September 11** **Also due today:** Ethics in Action CD-ROM (Part II and completion of the activities)
(5)	September 18 Week 5	**Chapter 4 Multicultural Perspectives and Diversity Issues** **Take-Home Quiz #4 on Chapter 4 due September 18** **ACA Video** (Part on Ethics in Multicultural Counseling)
(6)	September 25 Week 6	**Chapter 5 Client Rights and Counselor Responsibilities** **Informed Consent as Foundation of Counseling** **Take-Home Quiz #5 on Chapter 5 due September 25**
(7)	October 2 Week 7	**Chapter 6 Confidentiality: Ethical and Legal Issues** **ACA Video** (Informed Consent and Confidentiality) **Take-Home Quiz #6 on Chapter 6 due on October 2** **Self-Reflection Paper #1 due today**
(8)	October 9 Week 8	**Chapter 7 Boundary Issues and Multiple Relationships** **Due: Ethics in Action CD-ROM (Part III)** View all role-play vignettes and complete exercises in Part III **Take-Home Quiz #7 on Chapter 7 due on October 9** **Video: ACA Video:** Part on Dual Relationships
(9)	October 16 Week 9	**Boundary Issues and Multiple Relationships** [Continued] **Boundary Issues in Counseling: Multiple Roles** **Videos: Ethics in Action: Institutional Version (Part III)**
(10)	October 23 Week 10	**Chapter 8 Professional Competence and Training** **Training and Licensure Issues** **Take-Home Quiz #8 on Chapter 8 due on October 23**
(11)	October 30 Week 11	**Chapter 9 Ethics in Supervision and Consultation** **Ethical and Legal Issues in Supervision** **Take-Home Quiz #9 on Chapter 9 due on October 31**
(12)	November 6 Week 12	**Chapter 10 Issues in Theory, Practice and Research** **Ethics in Theory and Practice** **Take-Home Quiz #10 on Chapters 10 due on November 6** **Self-Reflection Paper #2 due on November 6**
(13)	November 13 Week 13	**Chapter 11 Ethical Issues in Couples and Family** and **Chapter 12 Ethical Issues in Group Counseling** **Take-Home Quiz #11 on Chapters 11+12 due on November 13**
(14)	November 20 Week 14	**Chapter 13 Ethical Issues in Community Work** Continue with **Ethical Issues in Group Work** **Take-Home Quiz #12 on Chapter 13 due on November 20**

NOVEMBER 25 to 29 FALL BREAK

(15)	December 4 Week 15	**Review of Highlights** Explore and discuss major learnings in course Retake the Self-Assessment (50-item inventory) in Chapter 1 and discuss in class.
(16)	December 11	**FINAL EXAMINATION WEEK (4:00-6:00)**

Final Exam consists of 100 items based on Chapters 1 to 13 of text. **Suggestions for preparing for final:** (1) Look at your CD-ROM at home one more time! (2) take again the Self-Assessment at end of Chap. 1; (3) carefully read and review Chaps. 1 to 13 of **Issues and Ethics**; (4) re-take the take-home quizzes for Chapters 1-13; and (5) take the practice examination and score this test.

Course Rationale

Although professional counselors need to operate under personal and professional codes of ethics, often these guidelines leave many questions unanswered. No single universally "right" answer exists for most ethical dilemmas. It is critical to be familiarized with the current professional, ethical, and legal issues that confront the counselor's role in a variety of settings. It is especially important to become sensitive to thinking about different ethical dilemmas and to learn decision-making strategies. Rather than arriving at one answer, what is important is to learn how to think through ethical issues in a systematic manner.

Course Objectives

1. To familiarize the student with ethical standards and practice.
2. To familiarize the student with ethical decision making models.
3. To examine the role of ethics and values in the counseling process.
4. To acquaint the student with various counselor roles and the potential for the development of ethical dilemmas.
5. To facilitate awareness of current professional issues.
6. To enhance the student's development of professional identity and its associated responsibilities.
7. To examine ways to establish appropriate boundaries and to develop a framework for evaluating and managing multiple relationships.
8. To examine the ethical decision-making process and its role in the counseling process.
9. To assist the student in examining, critiquing, and articulating her or his own ethical posture.

Course Competencies

1. The student will be able to respond to ethical dilemmas by a decision-making process.
2. The student will be able to communicate his or her value system, with emphasis on how these values are likely to impact counseling practice.
3. The student will be able to identify the different major components of ethical codes for professional counselors.
4. The student will be able to communicate how her/his personal values influence her/his ethical posture.
5. The student will be able to identify the professional organizations for counselors.

Focus of the Ethics Course

The class will <u>not</u> be a lecture class, rather it will be conducted more along the lines of a <u>seminar</u>. While some brief lectures will be given, the focus is upon discussion, interaction, role-playing, exploration of issues, and carrying out in class (and small groups) the <u>activities and exercises</u> at the end of each chapter. Come to class prepared!! Read, think, be willing to state your views, exchange ideas!!

PLEASE --- Disengage your cell phones!!!! No tape recordings allowed of any portions of this course!

Grading Practices and Policy

Your grade for this course will be determined by evidence of the quality of your learning as demonstrated by your performance on the following areas:

(1) TAKE HOME QUIZZES (12 of them at 5 points each for a total of 60 possible points); PARTICIPATION (which includes quality of participation in class discussions and attendance) = 40 points; Completing of exercises in Ethics in Action CD-ROM (50 points possible). **This is a possible 150** points for take-home quizzes, participation/attendance, and CD-ROM activities

(2) Self-Reflection Paper #1 (October 2) counts as 100 possible points

(3) Self-Reflection Paper #2 (November 6) counts as 100 possible points

(4) The FINAL EXAMINATION (Chapter 1-13)

Taking categories #1 to #4 above, there are 550 possible points, which will be converted into a percentage grade, using the scale below.

Grading Scale (percentage) is as follows:
100-98 = A+
97-94 = A
93-91 = A-
90-88 = B+
87-84 = B
83-81 = B-
80-78 = C+
77-74 = C
73-71 = C-
70-68 = D+
67-64 = D
63-61 = D-
Below 60 = F

Grade history (for your interest) is listed below. Over the 17 semesters this course has been offered, a total of 310 students have enrolled in HUSR 400, with the following grades earned:
A's = 81   (26%)
B's = 163   (53%)
C's = 53   (17%)
D's = 8   (3%)
F's = 5   (2%)

Class Participation
This course is organized in a seminar format and you are expected to participate in the class activities and discussions. **Your final course grade is likely to be affected by both the quality and quantity of your in-class participation and attendance.** I do expect you to function as a professional in any agency, which means showing up and participating! This also means arriving on time for the beginning of the class and after breaks, and staying for the full duration of the three-hour class. If this is a problem for you, please do not enroll in this section.

Attendance at full duration of class is expected at each class meeting, unless you have an emergency situation or are really ill. For me to credit you with an EXCUSED ABSENCE, you need to know that it is YOUR RESPONSIBILITY to inform me of such cases immediately upon returning to class -- or in advance is you know you will need to miss a class or a part of a class. **Absences and tardiness** will be a factor in determining your participation/attendance grade; unexcused absences or tardiness can result in getting a full grade deducted (or in some cases even failing the course). Absences are figured into the participation grade. **To be able to get credit for the quizzes, you must attend the class session.**

NOTE: Please bring to every class session both the **Issues and Ethics** text and the **COURSE OUTLINE** and **SYLLABUS**. Also, there may be a **READER** for both of your papers. I will still read your papers, however.

GUIDELINES FOR PAPERS FOR HUMAN SERVICES 400

PAPERS #1 and #2 makes up **50%** of your course grade. LATE PAPERS generally have a **penalty of at least** -15% deduction (if only a few days late) from the total. That means that if you were to receive a 93% for your paper, it would come out to 79% if it is late! The paper should be TYPED and double-spaced, CAREFULLY PROOFREAD, and should give evidence of considerable thought/outside reading, and must show a development of your positions in a coherent, logical, and organized way. Approximate length: **Each paper is to be 10 pages**. **IMPORTANT!** Put your name on the title page only, use no folder, and staple all ten essays (or ten pages) together.

There is a possibility that a READER will pre-read your papers before I do. I will discuss this possibility with you before you complete your papers. I will still read your papers, even if I have a reader.

SELF-REFLECTION PAPER #1 [Total of 10 pages]

Consider yourself as a future counselor or social worker, as you write your paper. The first paper focuses on: (1) Ethical decision making process (with emphasis on self-awareness and analysis of ACA Code of Ethics), (2) analysis of your values with implications for counseling practice, including role of cultural values in counseling, (3) Parts 1 and 2 of Ethics in Action CD-ROM, and (4) Issues and Ethics text, Chapters 1 to 6. The central theme of questions #4 to 8 deal with **VALUE ISSUES**. For these questions your task is to examine ways your values might affect your counseling practice, either positively or negatively. Use Chapter 3 of **Issues and Ethics** text (Values) as the core chapter, and also Part II of the **Ethics in Action CD-ROM (Part II on Values)**. Focus on ways that your values would influence the manner in which you think about ethical issues and how you would resolve an ethical dilemma.

Each of the following essays is to be limited to ONE PAGE. Begin each new essay on a separate page, number the question, and **use the title** at the top of your page, which is given in bold print below.

1. **Steps in Making Ethical Decisions.** (See Chapter 1, pages 18-22; and Part 1 of **Ethics in Action CD-ROM**). Select any ONE of the cases given in Chapters 3, 4, or 5 and demonstrate the steps you would take in dealing ethically with the situation.

2. **Countertransference.** Identify one form of countertransference you might struggle with and address how you would deal with this in an ethical manner. (Chapter 2)

SELECT EITHER 3a (Teen Pregnancy) or 3b (The Divorce) to write on:

3a. **Teen Pregnancy.** (See **Ethics in Action CD-ROM**, Part 1). Put yourself in the place of Suzanne's counselor. Address how you'd deal with her situation.

3b. **The Divorce.** (See **Ethics in Action CD-ROM**, Part 2). Put yourself in the place of Gary's supervisor. What points would you most want him to consider?

SELECT EITHER 4a (The Promiscuous One) or 4b (The Affair) to write on:

4a. **The Promiscuous One.** (See **Ethics in Action CD-ROM**, Part 2). Assume you are Suzanne's counselor. What issues would you consider in working with her? How would your values influence your interventions?

4b. **The Affair.** (See **Ethics in Action CD-ROM**, Part 2). Assume you are Natalie's counselor. What issues would you consider in working with her? How would your values influence your interventions?

5. **Dealing with a Value Conflict.** (See Chapter 3 and **Ethics in Action CD-ROM**). Identify one specific value that you are likely to push, or an area where you expect to struggle because of a value conflict with a given client. Or -- identify one of your core values and show how this value could either enhance or inhibit the effectiveness of counseling. Demonstrate how you might proceed to lessen the chances that you would impose your values on this client.

6. **Ethics in Multicultural Practice.** (See Chapter 4). Raise what you consider to be one of the MOST significant questions regarding the **ethical** aspects of multicultural practice – and then address your question.

7. **Multicultural Counseling Competencies.** (See Chapter 10, Chart on pages 138-139). After studying the areas of attitudes and beliefs, knowledge, and skills of a culturally skilled helper, what *specific areas* do you most need to work on to become effective in dealing with diversity? How might you go about acquiring multicultural competence?

8. **Malpractice.** (See Chapter 5, pages 180-190). Identify some of the ways you will go about decreasing the chances of getting involved in a malpractice suit. Focus on your attitudes and actions that are likely to prevent you from malpractice actions.

9. **Informed Consent.** (See Chapter 5, pages 149-163). Address how you are likely to go about the process of obtaining informed consent from a client during the initial session. What aspects would you most want to address? [Note: Do not include confidentiality in your answer, since this is question #9].

10. **Confidentiality**. [See Chapter 6]. What would you most want to tell your clients about confidentiality during the early sessions? Present some of your main ideas in simple and clear language, as though this were a part of your informed consent.

SELF-REFLECTION PAPER #2 [Total of 10 pages]

Consider yourself as a future counselor or social worker as you write your paper. Address your thoughts on the topics of multiple relationships by addressing the following specific questions.

Each of the following essays is to be limited to ONE PAGE. Begin each new essay on a separate page, number the question, and use the title given in bold print. And use a title page (with your name only on this cover sheet). Staple the paper together, but use no folder.

1. **Your Guidelines for Establishing Boundaries.** After studying the role-play vignettes in the Ethics in Action CD-ROM for Part 3, and doing the reading on managing boundaries and multiple relationships, write your own guidelines for how you will go about establishing clear and appropriate boundaries with clients.

SELECT EITHER 2a (The Picnic) or 2b (The Friendship) to write on:

2a. **The Picnic.** (See **Student Workbook** pages 60-62 and **Video**). Assume you are Lucia's counselor and she asks you to move her counseling sessions to the park. What are your thoughts? What would you tell her? What would you do, and why?

2b. **The Friendship.** (See **Student Workbook** pages 62-64 and **Video**; and see Chapter 7, pages 238-241). Assume that one of your clients is terminating and he or she lets you know he or she would like to begin some form of a social relationship. What issues would you explore with your client? Explain how you'd proceed.

SELECT EITHER 3a (Bartering) or 3b (Gift Giving) to write on:

3a. **Bartering**. (See The Architect, with Jerry/Janice in **Video and Workbook**, pages 68-72; and Chapter 7, pages 234-238). Your client tells you that he or she will have to terminate counseling with you because of losing a job and the inability to pay for therapy. Your client suggests a bartering arrangement with you as a way to continue therapy. Demonstrate how you'd deal with this situation in an ethical and effective manner. What specific issues would you want to address with this client?

3b. **Gift Giving.** (See Tickets for Therapy, with Marianne/John in Video and Student Workbook, pages 73-76). Create a BRIEF case where your client offers you a gift. What issues are you likely to explore with your client. What are your thoughts about accepting gifts from clients?

4. **Sexual Attractions**. (See The Disclosure, in **Ethics in Action CD-ROM**; and Chapter 7, pages 267-272). Assume that one of your clients informs you that he/she finds you sexually attractive. Show how you'd deal with this situation. What issues would you explore? What if you also found this client attractive? And what if you did not find this person attractive?

5. **Competence.** (See Chapter 8). What does it mean to you to be a competent professional? How will you assess your competence? How will you maintain your competence?

6. **Supervision**. (See Chapter 9). Assume you are an intern at an agency and you have a different point of view regarding how to deal ethically with a client. You are in conflict with your supervisor. Create a brief scenario and show how you'd address this issue with your supervisor?

7. **Your Theoretical Stance.** (See Chapter 10, pages 357-363). Write what you would most want to say to your clients, perhaps as a part of the informed consent process, about your theoretical stance and how your theoretical orientation influences the manner in which you practice.

8. **Diagnosis**. (See Chapter 10, pages 363-372). After reading about the arguments for and against diagnosis, as well as the authors' position on diagnosis, write your own position on diagnosis as you would explain it to your clients. What would you most want to say to your clients about your views on diagnosis?

9. **What You've Learned for Ethics in Action CD-ROM.** You have now completed Parts 1, 2, and 3 of the **Ethics in Action CD-ROM.** Discuss what you've most learned about *how to deal effectively* with ethical dilemmas. Please be concrete, specific, clear, concise, and hit the major points. This question asks you to summarize and conceptualize what you have learned about the process of making an ethical decision.

10. **Shifts in Your Thinking about Ethics.** (Retake the Self-Inventory: An Inventory of Your Attitudes and Beliefs about Professional and Ethical Issues – in Chapter 1 on pages 22-30). Write a page that clearly describes what you consider to be the most important shifts in your thinking about ethical practice (clarification of your views and beliefs, modifications in your thinking on a given issue, gaining new insights, or acquiring a new perspective). What have you **most learned** about yourself and/or about what constitutes becoming an ethical practitioner?

FURTHER SUGGESTIONS FOR YOUR SELF-REFLECTION PAPERS

Your task is to narrow down each of the above questions so that you have a clear focus. Take a definite position and develop it concisely and clearly -- and give logical reasons for your perspectives. To write outstanding papers, it will help to show evidence that you have read the relevant material in the main textbook and that you have done the reading on each issue in question -- and that you have viewed several times the **Ethics in Action CD-ROM** and that you have worked through the **Student Workbook** that accompanies the self-study video.

You are to develop your own position and back up these views with supporting evidence (either through your observations and experiences, or through key ideas in the readings). These are to be THOUGHT and REFLECTION PAPERS, not merely summary of information papers!! Take a SPECIFIC position, show why you take such a position, and then develop your viewpoints by giving reasons for the statements you make. Be creative in the way you approach this assignment.

The paper should be done in personal style and should reflect your study, review, and thought on given ethical and professional issues. In both papers, DO NOT write in global, abstract, and impersonal ways. Avoid writing about counselors or social workers in general or about counseling practice in general. Write about YOU as a future social worker or counselor and about concrete issues that you have conviction about.

You should know that you are not graded on your viewpoints and thoughts as such. Instead, your grade is a function of your ability to clearly, concisely, and fully express your ideas. I am looking for depth of thinking, originality, critical evaluation, the ability to apply key ideas and themes to practical situations, independent judgment, organization, and insights into issues. **Let your papers demonstrate that you are doing the reading and reflecting necessary to produce a quality paper.**

SUGGESTIONS FOR WRITING AND CRITERIA FOR GRADING

1. **Quality writing skills.** Write directly and informally, yet write in standard English. I encourage you to use personal examples and to support your points with these examples when appropriate. Make sure your essays reflect university-level writing skills. Use complete sentences, develop your paragraphs, check your spelling, and put together a paper that reflects quality. You might ask someone to proofread your paper. It is essential that you keep strictly within the established page limitations.

2. **Development of a theme.** Look for a central theme or central message in each essay. Make an outline, and check to see that each point in your outline pertains to your central message.
   - Create a short title for each section of your paper that conveys your basic idea.
   - State your message concisely in your opening paragraph in each of the three sections.
   - Have a solid and impactful concluding paragraph in each of the three sections.
   - The theme should be clear, concise, and specific -- rather than global and generalized. Do not write in a general and abstract manner, or else your essays will lose a clear focus.
   - Develop your thoughts fully, concretely, and logically -- rather than rambling or being vague and wordy.
   - In terms of form and organization, your paper should flow well, and your points should relate to one another. The reader should not have to struggle to discover and your intended meaning.
   - Give reasons for your views -- rather than making unsupported statements. In taking a position, provide reasons for your position.

- Cover a few issues or ideas well and in depth, rather than spreading yourself too thin. For each section of the paper, narrow down your particular topics so that you can manage to develop central paragraphs that expand on your theme.

3. **Use of examples.** In developing your ideas, use clear examples to illustrate your point. Draw upon personal examples, use cases, and apply ethical principles to practical work settings. Tie your examples into the point you are making -- but avoid giving too many details or getting lost in the personal example.

4. **Creativity and depth of thinking.** Write a paper that reflects your own uniqueness and ideas -- rather than merely giving a summary of the material in the book.
   - Do not make your papers mere summaries, rather focus on a clear position that you take on a specific question or issue.
   - Approach the material in an original way.
   - Focus on a particular issue or topic that you find personally significant. Since you have choice in what aspect to focus on, select an aspect of a problem that will allow you to express your beliefs.
   - Show depth in expanding on your thoughts.

5. **Integration and application.** Your papers should emphasize an integration of perspectives and an application of ethical principles and ethical reasoning to counseling practice.
   - Demonstrate that you know the material or the issues involved through an integration of the codes and the readings, accurate understanding of readings, critical evaluation of videos and readings, and ability to apply both readings and videos to practical situations.
   - Stress the implications of what you are writing for counseling practice with diverse client populations. Demonstrate how multicultural dimensions must be taken into consideration if you are to practice ethically.
   - Apply your ideas to specific populations that you expect to work with -- both in counseling and non-counseling situations. You may want to apply parts of your paper to teaching, working with the elderly, working in corrections, working with adolescents, etc. Make your paper a personal and meaningful experience by showing how you would apply ethical reasoning to dealing with ethical dilemmas that you are likely to encounter.
   - In writing about ethical issues, be sure to zero in on a specific message. What do you most want to convey?
   - In writing about a case, be sure to show that you can apply ethical principles and your knowledge of the ethics codes in discussing a case given in the **Issues and Ethics** book and the **Ethics in Action CD-ROM.** Work with the case by highlighting your knowledge of ethics as it applies to steps you might take if you were involved in a given case -- as a counselor, consultant, supervisor, or supervisee.

PART 3

STUDY GUIDE for
Issues and Ethics in the Helping
Professions, Sixth Edition

CHAPTER 1 Introduction to Professional Ethics

Ethical Decision Making
1. Be familiar with the meaning of the following terms and the differences among these terms: ethics, values, morality, community standards, laws, and professionalism.

2. What is the relationship between law and ethics? What might you do if you were faced with a conflict between a legal standard and an ethical principle?

3. Differentiate between mandatory ethics and aspirational ethics.

4. What is the role of professional codes? How do codes of ethics help counselors? What are the limitations of these codes?

5. What are the main objectives fulfilled by codes of ethics?

6. What are the differences between principle ethics and virtue ethics?

7. One model of ethical decision making is based on these six basic moral principles: autonomy, nonmaleficence, beneficence, justice, fidelity, and veracity. Be able to define each concept and provide an example for each principle.

8. Select an ethical dilemma and apply systematic steps to the resolution of the dilemma. Show the steps you might use in making an ethical decision. How might you include a client in making such a decision?

9. What are some of the advantages of including the client in the process of working through ethical decisions? Discuss the feminist model of ethical decision making, showing how some of the ideas of this model can lead to client empowerment.

10. If a professional disagrees with a particular ethical standard, and decides to practice in a way that is not sanctioned by an association, what are the consequences for that practitioner?

11. The text states that you need to develop an ethical sense that will enable you to better serve the welfare of your clients. What are some ways that you can think of to best develop this ethical sense?

CHAPTER 2 The Counselor as a Person and as a Professional

Self-Awareness and Influence of Therapist's Personality and Needs
1. How do unresolved personal conflicts affect the counselor's ability to work with clients?

2. What are some of your major motivations for you becoming a counselor? How might these motivations and needs be met through your work?

3. If you were asked the question "What do you personally get from doing counseling?", how would you answer this in a job interview?

Personal Therapy for Counselors
1. What is the rationale for the premise that therapy is essential for therapists and for trainees?

2. Do you think that personal therapy should be required of all trainees in a counseling program? If so, why? And what form of therapy do you think should be required?

3. To what extent should therapists make use of therapy for themselves? For those practitioners who are reluctant to seek professional assistance for themselves when they are highly stressed, what do you think might account for this reluctance?

4. Do you think that therapy should be *required* for an impaired therapist?

Dealing with Transference and Countertransference

1. How can transference and countertransference be ethical issues?

2. In what way is transference an "unreal" relationship in therapy?

3. When is countertransference a problem? If you were to become aware of countertransference reactions toward a particular client, what course of action would you likely follow?

4. Identify some of the major ways that countertransference is likely to be manifested. What are some of the signs that a therapist is experiencing countertransference?

Client Dependence and Manipulation
1. In what sense is promoting client dependence an ethical issue? What are some examples of fostering client dependence?

2. How can delaying termination of therapy be a form of client dependency?

3. How is manipulation an ethical issue? Could it be said that manipulation is really a part of every therapy approach?]

4. What are some ways that you can develop collaborative relationships with your clients?

Stress in the Counseling Profession
1. What are the major sources of stress for therapists?

2. In what sense can a career in counseling be a "hazardous profession?"

3. How does the stress of professional practice impact the counselor's personal life? What are the ethical issues here?

4. What are some of your concerns about your ability to cope with the stresses associated with being a professional?

5. What is your concept of the impaired therapist? What suggestions would you have if an impaired colleague sought you out for help?

6. What is your personal strategy for maintaining your vitality?

CHAPTER 3 Values and the Helping Relationship

Clarifying Your Values and Their Role in Your Work
1. Is it possible for counselors to keep their values out of their counseling sessions? What are the various views on this issue?

2. What are the ethics of imposing counselor values on clients?

3. Do you think that there are times or circumstances where it is ethical for you to direct clients in a particular direction? What about instilling in clients certain basic values such as responsibility, avoiding harm to others, being honest with others, self-determination, developing the ability to give and receive affection, finding a sense of purpose, and living authentically?

4. You will inevitably incorporate certain value orientations into your therapeutic practice. What is the ethical obligation you have in informing clients about your value orientation? How might you do this in your practice?

5. Is it possible for you, as a therapist, to interact honestly with your clients without making value judgments? Do you see it as desirable to avoid making judgments in all circumstances?

6. Can you remain true to yourself and at the same time allow your clients the freedom to select their own values, even if they differ sharply from yours?

7. At what point are counselors ethically obligated to refer a client because of a conflict of values? When would you feel it necessary to refer?

8. Do counselors need to share the same life experiences and world views of their clients to effectively work with them? If you have a background that is quite different from your client, how will you be able to make a connection with him or her?

Role of Spiritual and Religious Values in Counseling
1. Discuss the trend in the counseling profession that seems to be taking a stronger stand on incorporating spirituality and religion as a factor in assessment and treatment.

2. The premise of the authors is that spiritual and religious values have a major part to play in human life, which means that exploring these values has a great deal to do with providing solutions to the client's struggles. What is your reaction to this premise?

3. How would you expect your spiritual and religious values to affect the manner in which you counsel? Would you be inclined to introduce the topic of spirituality or religion if your client did not make specific mention of such factors, if you believed that doing so would be helpful?

4. What are some ways that religion and spirituality in counseling might conflict? In what ways can the two work in concert? What is the interface between the values espoused by religion and spirituality within the framework of counseling practice?

5. What are some reasons to include spiritual and religious values in counseling? What potential problems can you see with doing so?

6. What is the responsibility of training programs in preparing future counselors to deal with the religious and spiritual concerns of their clients?

7. What kind of competencies in spirituality do you think counselors should have by the end of their training?

End-of-Life Decisions
1. What are the ethical considerations in the right to die and in rational suicide?

2. If a person is able to make a free and rational choice about ending his or her life, do you think that the state should interfere in this choice?

3. What are some of the arguments for and against physician-assisted suicide? What is the possible role that a counselor might assume in such cases?

4. What is the essence of the NASW's policy on end-of-life decisions? To what extent do you support the client's self-determination in end-of-life decisions?

5. What are your values regarding clients exercising self-determination in the area of making end-of-life decisions? How might your values influence your interventions in such cases?

Values Pertaining to Sexuality
1. What are your values pertaining to sexuality? In what ways might your values in these areas either help or hinder you in making effective contact with clients? Can you think of any areas where you would have a tendency to push clients to make a certain decision with respect to sexual behavior?

2. If you were working with a couple, and if one person had been involved in an extramarital affair for some time, how might this affect your work with them?

CHAPTER 4 Multicultural Perspectives and Diversity Issues

The Need for a Multicultural Emphasis
1. Define each of the following terms: ethnicity, culture, minority group, multicultural, multicultural counseling, diversity, culturally encapsulated counselor, diversity-sensitive counseling, culture-centered counseling, racism, and stereotypes.

2. How is cultural tunnel vision sometimes a problem with mental health practitioners?

3. What are some steps you can take to deal effectively with cultural diversity and pluralism?

4. What are some reasons you can offer for the need for a multicultural emphasis in the practice of counseling?

Ethics Codes in Multicultural Counseling
1. What are the limitations of existing codes for multicultural counseling?

2. To what degree, if at all, is the ACA Code of Ethics and Standards of Practice and the APA Ethical Principles culturally biased and culturally encapsulated? What evidence is there in these codes that they are culturally sensitive?

3. What evidence is there that the NASW's Code of Ethics deals with diversity perspectives and multicultural concerns?

Cultural Values and Assumptions in Therapy

1. What are some of the main differences between Western and Eastern values? What are the implications of these differences for practice?

2. In what senses are contemporary theories of therapy and therapeutic practices grounded in Western assumptions?

3. What are some specific values associated with a Western orientation?

4. What are some specific values associated with an Eastern orientation?

5. What is one example of a stereotypic belief that you might hold toward a particular group? How might you challenge this belief?

6. How are a counselor's assumptions about self-disclosure pertinent in counseling certain ethnic groups? How about the counselor's assumptions about assertiveness? About self-actualization? About nonverbal behavior? About directness? About trusting?

Matching Client and Counselor

1. What are some factors that have a bearing on the question, Does a counselor have to share the racial and cultural backgrounds of the client to be effective?

2. What are your thoughts on the issue of matching client and counselor? In what areas do you think it is important to be matched with your client? How can you bridge any differences?

3. What is the basic difference between an intentional racist and an unintentional racist? In what way might you be an unintentional racist? What are some of the best ways of changing any unintentional racist attitudes or behaviors?

Multicultural Training for Counselors

1. Becoming a culturally aware therapist is not an either/or condition, but it is best considered on a continuum from being unaware of cultural issues to a heightened awareness of the role that cultural factors play in counseling. Where do you see yourself on this continuum? How aware are you of the cultural dynamics that enter into a therapeutic relationship? How comfortable do you feel in working with cultural differences that may emerge in helping relationships?

2. What are the main characteristics of the culturally skilled counselor?

3. What do you consider to be the essential components of multicultural counseling? Include a discussion of beliefs and attitudes, knowledge, and skills of culturally skilled counselors.

4. What are your thoughts on an ideal training program for multicultural counseling?

Ethical Issues in Counseling Gay, Lesbian, and Bisexual Clients

1. How might the values you hold either help or hinder your ability to establish effective relationships with lesbians or gay men?

2. What are the main ethical issues that you think need to be addressed pertaining to counseling gay and lesbian clients?

3. Some writers have suggested that the mental health profession has too often been insensitive to the needs of gay, lesbian, and bisexual clients. What are your thoughts on this matter?

4. What are some guidelines you could use in working with gay, lesbian, and bisexual clients?

5. Do you think that therapists should be ethically required to obtain specialized training in counseling gay and lesbian clients? If yes, what kind of training would you propose? If no, what are your reasons for not requiring this specialized training?

6. From your vantage point, what do you consider to be the special needs of gay, lesbian, and bisexual clients? How might you address these needs in your counseling?

7. For those counselors who believe that homosexuality is immoral, do you think that they have an ethical right to counsel gay, lesbian, or bisexual clients?

CHAPTER 5 Client Rights and Counselor Responsibilities

Client's Right to Give Informed Consent
1. How is informed consent a basic right of clients?

2. What are some common themes found in the various ethics codes pertaining to informed consent?

3. From a *legal* perspective, what are the three elements involved in adequate informed consent? Define these terms: capacity, comprehension of information, and voluntariness.

4. What are some of your ideas on how you would go about educating clients about informed consent?

5. If you were to create an informed consent document that you would give your clients, what are the main elements that would be contained in this document?

6. Do you think that your clients should have access to their files? Why or why not?

7. Do you think clients have a right to know their diagnostic classification? Why or why not?

The Counselor's Responsibilities in Record Keeping
1. What are the main points of the ethics codes pertaining to keeping records?

2. What is the main purpose of maintaining client records? What should be the general content of these records?

3. Are there any differences between the ethical and legal obligations pertaining to record keeping?

4. What is your stance on record keeping? What kind of records do you think would be most helpful?

Ethical Issues in the Counseling via the Internet
1. What are some advantages of counseling via the Internet?

2. What are some disadvantages of counseling via the Internet?

3. What are your thoughts about counseling via the Internet? What specific ethical issues do you think need to be raised? How comfortable would you be in using this form of technology in your counseling practice?

Counseling Children and Adolescents
1. What are some laws that you would need to be aware of if you were to work with minors?

2. How might you obtain informed consent of minors? Would you see children or adolescents without parental consent?

3. How might you explain resistance that you may get as you counsel reluctant children and adolescents? What are some possible meanings of this resistance, and how would you work with it?

4. Why is specialized training needed for those who counsel children and adolescents? What kind of training do you think is essential?

Involuntary Commitment and Human Rights
1. Before involuntarily committing a client, what would be some of the steps that you would take? What other courses of action would you take before you resorted to involuntary commitment procedures?

2. What are some of the major ethical and legal issues involved in the process of involuntary commitment?

Malpractice Liability in the Helping Professions
1. How would you define malpractice?

2. What does civil liability mean?

3. What constitutes professional negligence?

4. What is the meaning of the concept of standard of care?

5. What four conditions must be present in malpractice litigation? Define these four elements of malpractice: duty, breach of duty, injury, and causation.

6. What are the main grounds for malpractice suits? [What kind of violations have received the greatest attention in the literature?]

7. Be able to describe each of the following as a cause of malpractice suits:
   - failure to obtain informed consent
   - client abandonment
   - departing from established therapeutic practices
   - practicing beyond the scope of competency
   - misdiagnosis
   - unhealthy transference relationships
   - sexual abuse of a client
   - failure to control a dangerous client
   - managed care and malpractice
   - false memories

8. What has been the impact of malpractice litigation on practitioners?

9. What are some precautions that you would like take in dealing with high-risk clients?

10. What are some ways to protect yourself from malpractice suits? Identify specific safeguards and risk management strategies to lessen the chance of being successfully sued.

11. What course of action might you follow in a malpractice suit?

12. How do legal liability and ethical practice overlap at times?

CHAPTER 6 Confidentiality: Ethical and Legal Aspects

Confidentiality, Privileged Communication, and Privacy
1. Define these terms: confidentiality, privileged communication, and privacy. How are these related concepts? How is each term distinct?

2. How does privileged communication differ from confidentiality?

3. What ethical and legal ramifications of confidentiality would you want to present to your clients? What are the limits of confidentiality?

4. What limitations do you see on the confidentiality of the therapeutic relationship? When would you feel it necessary that confidentiality be compromised?

5. How might you educate your clients about the purposes and limits of confidentiality?

6. What are some ways that you might invade a client's privacy unintentionally?

7. What are some privacy issues you are concerned about with telephones, answering machines, voice mail, faxes, cellular phones, and e-mail?

Duty to Warn and Protect
1. What is involved in the therapist's duty to protect potential victims from dangerous acts of violent crimes?

2. What are the major implications of the Tarasoff case?

3. What was the ruling in the Bradley case?

4. What are the implications of the legal ruling in the Jablonski case?

5. What are the implications of the decision in the Hedlund case?

6. In what ways did the Jaffee case extend the confidentiality privilege?

7. What might be the consequences of the Jaffee case for licensed therapists and their clients?

8. How might your therapeutic practices be modified in light of your understanding of the above court cases?

9. What guidelines might you employ for dealing with dangerous clients? How might you go about making the determination of whether or not a person is potentially dangerous to self or others?

10. What are the ethical and legal duties to protect suicidal clients?

11. What are a few guidelines for assessing suicidal behavior?

12. What are the arguments in the case for suicide prevention?

13. What are the arguments in the case against suicide prevention?

14. What is your stance on the issue of suicide prevention?

15. What are the implications of duty to warn and to protect for school counselors?

Protecting Children From Harm
1. Once you suspect child abuse, what are you expected to do from both an ethical and a legal standpoint? Can you think of situations where what is ethical and what is legal might be in conflict in situations involving child abuse? What would you do if you experienced such a conflict?

2. What are your thoughts about the mandatory reporting laws of suspected cases of child or elder abuse?

3. Some believe that professionals should decide whether or not to report child abuse if their client is an offender, on the grounds that reporting could result in the end of therapy with this client. What do you think?

4. A review of some literature reveals that clinicians are hesitant to report suspected child abuse unless they are fairly certain that abuse is currently occurring. Do you think that ethical practice demands that practitioners report abuse, regardless of how long ago it occurred?

5. How do you distinguish abuse from harsh punishment? What cultural factors might enter into this assessment?

Confidentiality and HIV/AIDS-Related Issues
1. What do you see your ethical responsibilities as being with respect to educating yourself about the problems involved in working with HIV- positive clients and with persons with AIDS?

2. What are some of the common fears and misconceptions associated with HIV and AIDS? As a professional, what responsibilities, if any, do you think you have in educating the public about the disease?

3. What are the ethical issues involved in either maintaining or breaching confidentiality with clients who are HIV-positive and who are sexually active? Do you think you have a duty to warn and to protect identified third parties? What are the legal considerations in these situations?

4. How might an HIV-positive client who refuses to inform his or her partner of his or her status, a matter related to duty to warn and protect?

5. Do Tarasoff principles apply in AIDS-related psychotherapy?

6. What are the ethical implications, if any, involved in dealing with clients who have tested positive for HIV? What rights do your clients have who are HIV-positive? What are the rights of their partners? How do you balance the rights of both parties?

7. What key issues do you think are involved in considering the handling of confidentiality in HIV and AIDS-related therapy cases? What are some of the main ethical and legal considerations in these cases?

8. From an ethical perspective, what kind of special training on HIV-related issues should counselors receive?

CHAPTER 7 Managing Boundaries and Multiple Relationships

Dual/Multiple Relationships in Perspective

1. What is the definition of dual relationships? of multiple relationships? What are some of the more common forms of dual/multiple relationship?

2. Some writers focus on the problems inherent in dual/multiple relationships. Mention some of these problems that are associated with dual/multiple relationships.

3. Are all dual/multiple relationships necessarily unethical? Why or why not?

4. Some claim that dual or multiple relationships are inherent in the work of all helping professions, that they are not necessarily harmful, and that there may be some beneficial aspects to some dual relationships. What do you think of this perspective?

5. Some hold that dual/multiple relationships are inevitable and unavoidable, and that it is the responsibility of the professional to find ways to monitor the risks and safeguard clients. What are your reactions to this view?

6. What are the reasons that ethics codes caution practitioners against engaging in dual/multiple relationships?

7. What are some issues to consider in determining the degree to which dual/multiple relationships pose problems or raise the potential for harm to clients?

8. The case is often made that dual or multiple relationships often lead to a misuse of power and the exploitation of a client. Do you think these actions are necessarily linked to the existence of dual or multiple relationships? Why or why not?

9. Dr. Arnold Lazarus takes the position that certain boundaries and ethics actually diminish therapeutic effectiveness. He believes that some well-intentioned guidelines can backfire and that rather than being driven by rules that it is best for therapists to engage in a process of negotiation in many multiple relationships. What do you think about his views?

10. What ways can you monitor yourself pertaining to decisions to engage in any form of dual or multiple relating with clients? What kinds of safeguards can you think of to protect clients if you are involved in an unavoidable dual or multiple relationship?

11. What are some differences between boundary crossings and boundary violations?

12. What is your understanding of the term "role blending?" Can you think of ways that you might blend roles in your professional practice?

13. What relationship do you see between boundaries in your personal life and your ability to establish appropriate professional boundaries? What guidelines can you think of in establishing appropriate boundaries? In what areas, if any, might you expect to have difficulties in managing boundaries in the work setting?

Bartering for Professional Services

1. What do the ethics codes state about bartering?

2. When is bartering problematic? Why do some contend that bartering of services and goods for therapy services raises ethical concerns? What cultural factors need to be taken into account in determining whether to barter?

3. What are some arguments both for and against the practice of bartering for therapeutic services?

4. If a client were unable to pay for your services, would you be inclined to consider bartering if the client initiated this as a solution? If yes, what guidelines would you want to establish between you and your client? If you would not be willing to engage in bartering, what alternatives, if any, might you suggest?

Giving or Receiving Gifts

1. If a client offered you a gift, what would you say or do? What factors would you take into consideration in making a decision about accepting or not accepting the gift?

2. Can you ever think of an instance where you might give a gift to a client? Explain.

Social Relationships with Clients

1. What are the potential problems in situations where there is a blending of both personal and professional relationships? Do social relationships of any form necessarily interfere with therapeutic relationships? Explain.

2. When do you think that social relationships with *current* clients are unethical? What about the ethics of forming personal or social relationships with *former* clients?

3. Some counselors take the position that counseling and friendship should not be mixed. The argument is that blending social relationships with professional ones simultaneously can negatively affect the therapy process, the friendship, or both. What are your ideas about this viewpoint?

4. Some peer counselors might claim that friendships before or during counseling are actually positive factors in establishing trust and a productive therapeutic relationship. What do you think?

Sexual Attraction in the Client/Therapist Relationship
1. What are your thoughts on the matter of sexual attractions in the client/therapist relationship? To what extent have you thought about or discussed this topic?

2. If a client was attracted to you and expressed this, what do you think you would do? What if you were attracted to a client? What might you do or say?

3. What kind of education and training do you think graduate programs should include for trainees on the matter of learning how to deal effectively with sexual attractions?

4. If you were designing a training program to help counselor trainees learn how to recognize and effectively deal with sexual attractions in therapy, what would your program look like?

Sexual Relationships: Legal and Ethical Issues
1. In your education and training, what kind of information have you been given pertaining to sexual activity in a professional relationship?

2. Under what practices does touching tend to lead to intercourse in the therapy relationship?

3. What do the studies show concerning the frequency of sexual contact with clients?

4. What do the ethical standards say about sexual relationships with *current* client? with *former* clients?

5. What are the reasons that sexual intimacy between therapist and client is considered unethical and unprofessional?

6. What are some common misconceptions that tend to influence the therapist's decision to engage in sexual intimacies with a client?

7. What are the harmful effects of sexual intimacy on clients?

8. What are some legal sanctions against sexual violators? What are some ethical sanctions?

9. What kind of educational activities do you think training programs need to offer students in the helping professions?

10. What are the ethical and legal aspects of therapists forming either social or romantic relationships with *former* clients? What specific factors need to be addressed by therapists before they get involved in any personal way with *former* clients? Do you think it is ever justified, regardless of the amount of time elapsed since termination, for a therapist to form a sexual relationship with a former client? Explain your position.

11. Under what circumstances might you be inclined to report unethical behavior of a colleague?

12. What are the arguments for and against the use of touching in therapy? What are your thoughts pertaining to touch in the therapeutic relationship? What guidelines can you think of to help you make decisions on this matter?

CHAPTER 8 Professional Competence and Training Issues

Therapist Competence: Ethical and Legal Aspects
1. What are your thoughts on how you could determine your own level of competence?

2. What are the major ethical and legal issues related to therapist competence?

3. How might you know when to refer a client because of limited competence? In such a case, how would you go about making this referral? What would you do if a client refused to accept your referral?

4. What are a few ethical issues in the training of therapists?

Ethical Issues in Training Therapists
1. If you were a part of a screening committee to determine which candidates would be admitted to a counselor-training program, how would you best go about assessing a candidate's personal characteristics? What other factors would you want to use in screening applicants for a counselor-preparation program?

2. What do you think should be taught in preparing counselors for practice?

3. What are your thoughts about the assumption that training programs need to be designed so that students can learn a good deal more about themselves as well as acquire theoretical knowledge?

4. How do you think practitioners can best be trained? What are your thoughts on the training of therapists?

5. What are your thoughts regarding evaluating a trainee's personality, interpersonal behaviors, and performance?

6. What should the criteria be for graduating from a master's or doctoral program in counseling? How can the evaluation process of trainees best be handled?

7. What responsibility do you think a training program has to dismiss from the program a student who is psychologically or academically not able to perform satisfactorily in an internship? What kind of process would you recommend for providing feedback to such a student?

Professional Licensing and Credentialing
1. Define the following terms: registration, licensure, certification.

2. Does professional licensing indicate professional competence? Give reasons for your answer.

3. What are the purposes of legislative regulation of professional practice?

4. What are the arguments for and against professional licensing and credentialing?

5. The process of licensure, certification, credentialing, and registration can promote a sense of professional identity. It can also lead to professional jealousy over turf battles and interprofessional bickering. What are your views on the process of regulation of professional practice?

Continuing Education and Demonstration of Competence
1. What are your views on continuing education as a way to maintain competence? Are you in favor of requiring continuing education as a condition for relicensure?

2. How can peer review be a means of ensuring quality?

3. What value do peer-consultation groups have for counselors-in-training? for experienced practitioners?

CHAPTER 9 Issues in Supervision and Consultation

Ethical and Legal Issues in Clinical Supervision
1. In what ways are supervisors responsible, both ethically and legally, for the actions of their trainees?

2. What are the main roles and responsibilities that counseling supervisors have toward supervisees?

3. Because supervisors are expected to be knowledgeable regarding ethical, legal, and regulatory aspects of the profession, what kind of special training do you think supervisors need to function effectively?

4. From your perspective, what are the personal characteristic of an effective supervisor? What specific personal characteristics would you most want in your supervisor?

5. Which do you consider to be the proper focus of the supervision process --- the client or the counselor?

6. What is the role of informed consent in the supervision process? As a supervisee, what kind of information have your supervisors provided you with regarding what they expected of you? What, if anything, would you have wanted to know from your supervisor about the supervisory process or supervisory relationship?

7. Some consider negligent supervision to be fertile grounds for malpractice action. From your perspective, what constitutes negligence in supervision?

8. What are some other legal aspects pertaining to supervision? What is the difference between direct liability and vicarious liability?

Competence of Supervisors
1. What do you think constitutes a competent supervisor? What kinds of experiences do supervisors need to be competent? How do you think a supervisor's competence can best be assessed or determined?

2. From both an ethical and a legal perspective, why is competence a main element in supervision? Does possession of an advanced degree imply that a counselor can also supervise effectively? Does competence as a therapist necessarily imply competence as a supervisor? Explain.

Multicultural Issues in Supervision
1. What are the dimensions of a good model of multicultural supervision?

2. What kind of understanding of racial and ethnic diversity issues is essential for supervisors? What are some of the main issues regarding multicultural supervision?

3. What are your thoughts regarding ways of making supervision more multiculturally sensitive and effective?

4. What kind of training and supervision are required to achieve multicultural competence on the part of supervisees?

5. What importance do you place on gender issues in supervision?

6. What is the essence of feminist supervision? What are some of the guiding principles of feminist supervision?

Multiple Roles and Relationships in the Supervisory Process
1. When might dual or multiple relationships in the supervision process become an ethical issue? What are some examples of such relationships that you think are most problematic?

2. Most training programs in the helping professions involve educators playing more than one role. Educators and supervisors often engage in role blending to carry out their functions. What are your thoughts about ways to ethically manage training that frequently uses both didactic and experiential approaches?

3. Sexual intimacies between supervisors and supervisees pose several problems. What problems can you think of in such situations?

4. What are your thoughts about supervisors who combine supervision with personal counseling, especially in cases where a supervisee's personal problems are interfering with providing effective counseling?

5. What are the ethics involved of educators who counsel their current students? What about educators or supervisors who eventually accept a former student or supervisee as a client in therapy?

6. If you were a supervisor, what kind of boundaries would you want to establish with your supervisees?

7. As a student, have you encountered any problems pertaining to multiple roles and relationships with your professors or supervisors? How comfortable are you in learning to manage certain multiple roles and relationships from the perspective of a student?

8. If you were a supervisor, what would you want to tell your supervisees about what kinds of multiple roles and relationships are ethically problematic? about those multiple roles and relationships that may be beneficial or inevitable?

Ethical and Professional Issues in Consultation
1. How is consultation defined? What are the targets of the consultation process? What are the aims of the consultation process?

2. Why is a code of ethics needed for consultants?

3. What are some of the important ethical principles for consultants?

4. What are some unique dual relationship problems confronting consultants?

5. What kind of training do you think consultants need to function competently?

6. What are some examples of dual relationships in the consulting process? In what way can these relationships be problematic for both the consultee and the consultant?

7. From an ethical standpoint, what do you think consultants should know about an organization before they agree to enter into a contract with a particular group?

8. How are hidden agendas a particular problem in the practice of consulting?

9. If a consultant were to discover that the members of a particular organization were in need of personal therapy, what do you think is the consultant's responsibility?

10. How is consultation with colleagues a good practice throughout one's professional career?

CHAPTER 10 Issues in Theory, Practice, and Research

Developing a Counseling Stance
1. How would you describe your counseling stance? What are your assumptions about the nature of counseling and the nature of people?

2. How does your theoretical orientation affect your view of practice? In what way might your theoretical views become an ethical issue?

The Division of Responsibility in Therapy
1. In what way is therapy a joint venture of both the client and the therapist?

2. What are your thoughts on the division of responsibility in the therapeutic relationship?

3. Under what circumstances might this division of responsibility become an ethical concern?

Deciding on the Goals of Counseling
1. What do you consider to be a few of the most important goals of counseling?

2. Who is in the best position to determine therapeutic goals? Explain.

3. In what way might the process of deciding on goals for therapy become an ethical issue?

The Use of Techniques in Counseling and Therapy
1. What are the main ethical issues regarding the appropriate and ethical use of techniques?

2. In what situations is it likely that techniques could be abused?

3. What are the ethical issues involved in adapting techniques to the needs of the client?

4. What are your guidelines for using techniques in an ethical way?

Diagnosis as a Professional Issue
1. What is the main purpose of the diagnostic approach?

2. What does differential diagnosis mean?

3. What are the main arguments for psychodiagnosis?

4. What are the main arguments against psychodiagnosis?

5. What are some potential ethical issues associated with the process of diagnosis?

6. If you worked in an agency that required you to formulate a diagnosis and a treatment plan based upon this diagnosis at the initial session, how would this influence your practice?

7. What is the role of a client's ethnic and cultural background as it pertains to the process of diagnosis?

8. What is your position on psychodiagnosis?

9. What are some possible ethical issues surrounding diagnostic practices? Can you think of any unethical diagnostic practices?

10. What are some possible legal issues surrounding diagnostic practices?

Using Tests in Counseling
1. What guidelines would help you decide when you might want to use tests for counseling purposes?

2. What are some main ethical considerations in using tests?

3. In interpreting test results to a client, how would you take into consideration his or her ethnicity and cultural background?

4. What are some multicultural considerations in using tests?

Counseling in a Managed Care Environment
1. How did managed care come about?

2. What are some of the key differences between the fee-for-service system of private practice and the newer system of managed care?

3. Identify some of the main advantages and disadvantages of the managed care system, for both the client and the therapist? How can clients best be served given the limited mental-health resources?

4. What are some of the main ethical issues associated with managed care?

5. If you were working in a managed care setting, how would you handle informed consent with your clients? What would you most want them to know?

6. If you were working in a managed care setting, how would you handle the topic of confidentiality with your clients?

7. If you were working in a managed care setting, how might you deal with a client who was no longer entitled to services, yet you clearly believed that this person required further treatment? Do you have any thoughts about how you might deal with potential issues surrounding abandonment of a client?

8. What potential malpractice issues can you see associated with managed care policies and practices?

Ethical Issues in Psychotherapeutic Research
1. How is informed consent an ethical issue in research?

2. Do you think that it is ever justified to use deception in psychological research?

3. What are some potential ethical issues involved in situations involving withholding of treatment for experimental purposes?

4. Some writers have criticized the ethics codes of both ACA and APA on the grounds that they are not responsive and relevant to the pragmatic research needs of minorities. What are your thoughts on this topic?

CHAPTER 11 Ethical Issues in Couples and Family Therapy

Ethical Standards in Couples and Family Therapy
1. What are some ethical standards that are specific to the practice of couples and family therapy?

2. What are a few key ethical problems that face family therapists?

Contemporary Professional Issues
1. What are the major personal characteristics needed for an effective family therapist?

2. What are the educational requirements of marital and family therapists, according to the AAMFT?

3. What are the main standards of training and clinical experience?

4. What is the rationale for expecting family therapists to experience their own personal therapy and to work with their family of origin?

Values in Couples and Family Therapy
1. In what ways do the therapist's values take on special significance in counseling couples and families?

2. What are some areas where you might have difficulty in counseling families because of your values?

Gender-Sensitive Couples and Family Therapy
1. How are gender-role stereotypes a special concern for therapists who work with couples and families? How might your own values pertaining to traditional and nontraditional family arrangements influence your practice with couples and families?

2. How are gender stereotypes problematic in counseling both men and women?

3. When do the gender stereotypes of counselors become an ethical issue?

4. What are some ways of becoming a nonsexist family therapist? How can you use the therapeutic process to challenge the oppressive consequences of stereotyped roles and expectations in the family?

5. What are your thoughts on what constitutes gender-aware therapy?

6. What are some of the key concepts of the feminist approach to family therapy?

Responsibilities of Couples and Family Therapists
1. What are some special responsibilities of couples and family therapists?

2. When is it necessary to consult in this area of therapy?

Confidentiality and Informed Consent in Couples and Family Therapy

1. What are the exceptions to confidentiality as it applies to counseling with couples and families?

2. If you were working with a couple, what would you tell them from the outset about confidentiality?

3. If you were working with a family, what would you tell each member of that family from the outset about confidentiality?

4. How is confidentiality a special issue in couples and family therapy? What are some issues pertaining to confidentiality that a family therapist needs to clarify from the outset with each family member? What problems might you have in this area if you were to work with a family?

Informed Consent in Couples and Family Therapy
1. How is informed consent a special consideration in couples and family therapy?

2. If you were going to work with a couple, what would you most want them to know about how you conduct couples counseling?

3. If you were going to work with a family, what are some things you would most want each of the family members to know about how you view family therapy? What might you expect of them? What could they expect of you?

4. What are some issues involved in cases where therapists require attendance by all the members of a family as a condition for family therapy?

5. What are your thoughts about conducting a family therapy session without all the members of the family being present?

CHAPTER 12 Ethical Issues in Group Work

Training and Supervision of Group Leaders
1. What are some kinds of knowledge and skills you think are essential for effective group counselors? What about supervised experience in group work?

2. What are some of the main provisions of the *Professional Standards for the Training of Group Workers*? What do you think about different standards of training for the various group work specialties?

3. What kind of training program in group counseling would you like to participate in? What can you do to get the training in group work you are likely to need?

Co-Leadership
1. Ethically, when would you feel ready to lead or to co-lead a group in a community agency?

2. What ethical issues can you identify as they relate to co-leadership practices? Mention some advantages and disadvantages of the co-leadership model?

3. What qualities would you look for in selecting a co-leader?

Ethical Issues in Group Membership
1. In recruiting members for a group, what would you want to tell members before they made the decision to join a group?

2. What are some ethical issues involved in screening and selecting group members? How do you decide whom to include and exclude? Are there any ethical alternatives when screening is not practical or possible?

3. What kind of preparation and orientation would you want to provide for members in a group you would lead?

4. Should group membership always be voluntary? Are there any situations in which it is ethical to require participation in a group?

5. Once members make a commitment to be a part of a group, do they have the right to leave at any time they choose?

6. What are a few of the major psychological risks in group participation? What could you do to minimize these risks?

Confidentiality in Groups
1. What are the main ethical, legal, and professional issues pertaining to confidentiality in group situations?

2. As a group leader, how would you teach your members about confidentiality? How would you encourage confidentiality?

3. When, and under what circumstances, would you breach confidentiality in a group?

4. If you were leading a group with minors, what would you want to say to the members of your group about confidentiality? Would you require parental consent for children or adolescents to be in your group? Do parents have a right to information that is disclosed by their children in a group? Explain.

5. What kind of ethical issues surround group therapy over the Internet? What are the implications for confidentiality in Internet group therapy?

Values in Group Counseling
1. How can a group leader's values influence the group process? What is the ethical way a leader can use his or her values without imposing them on members?

2. What ethical issues are involved in members pressuring other members to adopt a particular value stance or to make a decision of how to live?

Diversity Issues in Group Work
1. In the text, the statement is made: "It is critical that leaders become aware of their biases based on age, disability, ethnicity, gender, race, religion, and sexual orientation." What personal meaning does this statement have for you?

2. What specific characteristics do you need to become a diversity competent group counselor?

3. What are a few guidelines for competence in diversity issues in group work?

Uses and Abuses of Group Techniques
1. What are some guidelines to avoid abusing techniques in a group?

2. How is therapist competence an ethical issue as it pertains to using group techniques?

3. What are some ethical concerns pertaining to using group techniques with culturally diverse client populations?

The Consultation and Referral Process

1. What are some ethical guidelines pertaining to the consultation and referral process as it pertains to group work? In what cases would you seek consultation in your work as a group leader?

2. When might you make a referral of a member to another professional?

3. What responsibilities do leaders have in suggesting ways members might continue engaging in personal change once they have completed a group? What kind of knowledge about resources is needed?

Issues Concerning Termination

1. What ethical and practical issues would you be concerned with as a group moves toward termination?

2. What kind of follow-up might you design for a group you have led?

CHAPTER 13 Ethical Issues in Community Work

The Community Mental-Health Orientation

1. What is a definition of community counseling?

2. What are some of the main ethical responsibilities you have to the community and to society?

3. What are the four main activities that make up a comprehensive community-counseling program?

4. How does the community mental-health approach differ from the traditional approach to therapy?

Roles of Counselors Working in the Community

1. Within the community perspective, what is the professional's role in educating the community?

2. What is the community worker' responsibility in the area of influencing policymakers?

3. What are the main goals of the outreach approach? What are some strategies of this approach?

4. What is the meaning of being an advocate for clients? What are some examples of counselors assuming the role of client advocate?

5. Describe each of the following alternative roles counselors might play in working in the community: change agent, consultant, adviser, advocate, facilitator of indigenous support system, and facilitator of indigenous healing system.

6. If you were to work in the community, what ideas do you have about ways you could become involved in that community?

The Use of Nonlicensed Workers

1. What is the reason for the increasing use of non-licensed workers in the human service field?

2. What are the types of non-licensed workers that are involved in human services?

3. What are some training standards that are needed for paraprofessionals and non-licensed workers?

4. What implications does the trend toward the use of paraprofessionals and non-licensed workers have upon the roles professionals will assume?

Working within a System

1. How has the emergence of case management become a dominant force in human services delivery?

2. What are some of the goals of the case management approach?

3. What are some of the ethical issues associated with case management as a way to deliver human services in a community agency?

4. How do you think you could retain a sense of vitality and integrity, while working within the boundaries of a system? How does this become an ethical issue?

5. What do you see as your relationship as a counselor to the agency where you work?

6. What are some ways that you can deal with the tendency to avoid responsibility by blaming the institution or system where you work?

7. What strategies can you think of for not getting lost in the system, yet for attaining your own professional goals? How might you assume power within the system?

PART 4

CHAPTER QUIZZES for
Issues and Ethics in the Helping Professions,
Sixth Edition

Directions: The questions below are divided into the following three areas. 1. Fact (F), referring to a questions that pertain to definitional or objective information. 2. Conceptual (C), in which the question is based on information generalized from particular instances and requires the student to interpret their responses. 3. Applied (A), based on case studies in which the response tests for the student's ability to apply theory to practical instances. The alphabetical letter is followed by the page number in which the test question was derived. (Only the first page number is used where two pages were needed to comprise the question.)

CHAPTER 1 INTRODUCTION TO PROFESSIONAL ETHICS

F-11   1. _____ is concerned with perspectives of right and proper conduct and involves an evaluation of actions on the basis of some broader cultural context or religious standard.

     a.   Ethical conduct
     b.   Community standards
     c.   Morality
     d.   Professionalism

A-11   2. Robert runs into the office, unprepared and frustrated because he is late for his weekly appointment with his first client of the day. He is consistently late for his appointments and his behavior is:

     a.   immoral.
     b.   illegal.
     c.   unethical.
     d.   unprofessional.

A-9   3. James and Mary were going to counseling for marital problems and the counselor decided to meet each partner in an individual session before meeting them as a couple. James confided that he was HIV-positive and was not going to tell his spouse because she would know that he had been unfaithful. The counselor decided to break confidentially after attempts to encourage James to inform his wife of his condition. The counselor's action:

     a.   was illegal and may result in sanctions.
     b.   may be considered ethical, yet the practitioner could be in violation of a legal standard.
     c.   was unethical since confidentiality was broken.
     d.   was ethical and meets the American Counseling Association standard regarding contagious diseases which states that practitioners must report when a client is HIV positive.

A-12   4. Elizabeth is a beginning practitioner and is counseling in a manner where she merely acts in compliance with the law and follows minimal ethical standards. She is at the first level of ethical functioning which is:

     a.   personal ethics.
     b.   aspiration ethics.
     c.   mandatory ethics.
     d.   basic ethics.

C-7   5. The basic purpose of professional code of ethics is to:

     a.   educate professionals about sound ethical conduct, provide a mechanism for professional accountability and serve as a catalyst for improving practice.
     b.   protect professionals from lawsuits.
     c.   set standards that will be understood and enforced across all cultures.
     d.   ensure that standards remain consistent over time.

A-10   6. A formal complaint was filed against Harry for sexually harassing a female client. This is not the first complaint against him and he was previously warned that a major sanction would be imposed if he continued his unethical actions. The professional ethics committee to which he belongs recommended that Harry:

    a.   be on probation during his entire career.
    b.   resign from his job.
    c.   work without supervision on his word that he will not harass any client again.
    d.   be expelled from the organization.

C-13   7. The counselor who asks the questions "Am I doing what is best for my client?" rather than "Is this situation unethical?" is functioning from the following ethical perspective:

    a.   principle ethics
    b.   virtue ethics
    c.   value ethics
    d.   practical ethics

C-14   8. The virtuous professional:

    a.   is motivated to do what is right because they feel obligated.
    b.   functions within their professional code of ethics because they fear the consequences if they do not.
    c.   possess vision and discernment, which involves sensitivity, judgment, and understanding and leads to decisive ethical actions.
    d.   typically focus on moral issues with the goals of solving a particular dilemma.

A-16   9. Richard is counseling a male Asian client and is encouraging him to go away to college even though he is expected to take care of his aging parents. Richard is violating the following basic moral principle in making ethical decisions:

    a.   nonmaleficence
    b.   autonomy
    c.   beneficence
    d.   fidelity

A-17   10. Jan is an incest victim and is covered for six sessions by insurance. Her counselor is in private practice and knows that Jan needs more sessions. She decides to offer Jan her services pro bono. In making the ethical decision to ensure that her client has equal access to services, the counselor is using the basic moral principal of:

    a.   fidelity.
    b.   justice.
    c.   beneficence.
    d.   veracity.

CHAPTER 2 THE COUNSELOR AS A PERSON AND AS A PROFESSIONAL

A-36   1. Rhonda is a counselor at a drug and alcohol treatment center. She grew up in an alcoholic home and is not fully aware of the "unfinished business" she has with her parents. She is still angry and resentful with her parents for growing up in an alcoholic family system. It is most likely that Rhonda will:

    a.   be able to understand her addicted clients through her own childhood experiences.
    b.   examine her unresolved conflicts as she continues to work in the treatment center.
    c.   obstruct the progress of her clients as they attempt to move towards recovery.
    d.   feel comfortable with her clients because she is familiar with their behavior.

C-38   2. Ronald directs his clients toward solutions instead of encouraging them to seek alternatives for themselves. He is likely to have a strong need:

    a.   for approval.
    b.   to feel a sense of achievement and accomplishment.
    c.   to empower his client.
    d.   to nurture his client.

C-38   3. Counselors who have unresolved personal conflicts:

    a.   need to recognize that their problems may interfere with their effectiveness and refrain from activities that would harm a client.
    b.   must resolve all their difficulties before counseling others.
    c.   are quite effective because they know how difficult it is to resolve problems.
    d.   need to repress anxiety-provoking issues in their own lives before becoming effective counselors.

F-46   4. _____ is the process whereby clients place past feelings or attitudes they had toward significant people in their lives onto their therapist.

    a.   Transference
    b.   Countertransference
    c.   Projection
    d.   Mirroring

C-55   5. Termination of the therapy process:

    a.   can be mandated by ethics codes alone.
    b.   is regulated by state law.
    c.   rests on the honesty and goodwill of the therapist.
    d.   must always be decided solely by the therapist.

C-48   6. Countertransference can be constructive in the therapeutic relationship when the therapist:

    a.   is overprotective with the client.
    b.   treats clients in benign ways.
    c.   recognizes transference patterns and can help the client change old dysfunctional themes.
    d.   over identifies with the client's problems.

A-48   7. Joanne finds herself wanting to solve her client's problems which are similar to the issues her daughter is going through. Joanne gives advice and feels frustrated when her client won't follow through on her suggestions. Her emotional reactions to her client, which involve her own projections is based on:

    a.   transference.
    b.   nurturance.
    c.   countertransference.
    d.   caretaking.

C-50   8. When counselors become overly concerned with meeting their own needs or pushing their own personal agendas, their behavior becomes:

    a.   annoying to the client.
    b.   unethical.
    c.   illegal.
    d.   narcissistic.

C-52   9. Sexual or romantic feelings toward a client:

    a.   is the result of seductive behavior on the part of the client and needs to be ignored.
    b.   is an indicator that the client needs to be referred to another counselor.
    c.   are unethical, counter therapeutic, and also illegal in many states.
    d.   does not necessarily mean that the counselor cannot effectively work with the client.
    e.   never occurs if the counselor is operating within their professional code of ethics.

C-59   10. Deutsch and Farber found surprisingly similar results in their surveys of therapists' perceptions of stressful client behavior. In both studies therapists reported that the following clients' behavior was <u>most</u> stressful for them:

       a.   aggression and hostility
       b.   suicidal statements
       c.   severely depressed clients
       d.   premature termination of therapy
       e.   agitated anxiety

CHAPTER 3 VALUES AND THE HELPING RELATIONSHIP

C-72   1. In regards to values in the counseling process, the authors contend that:

       a.   it is incumbent that counselor clarify their values and the ways in which they enter the therapeutic process.
       b.   counselors can avoid communicating values to their clients by not explicitly sharing them.
       c.   it is best to keep values hidden so they won't contaminate their client's choices.
       d.   their job to help clients conform to socially acceptable standards.

A-77   2. Mary is seeking abortion counseling from a practitioner who has been actively involved in the pro-life movement. The therapist has extreme discomfort with Mary's values and doesn't think he could maintain objectivity. It would be best if he:

       a.   doesn't share his values with Mary and work within the value system of his clients.
       b.   help Mary to understand his values so she can make a different decision concerning her pregnancy.
       c.   refers Mary to a therapist who shares the client's values.
       d.   set firm boundaries with Mary on what she can discuss in regards to her pregnancy.

F-86   3. _____ refers to a personal inclination or desire for a relationship with the transcendent on God.

       a.   Religion
       b.   Spirituality
       c.   Faith
       d.   Belief

C-93   4. The following is true regarding spiritual and religious values in counseling:

       a.   Clients can gain insight into the ways that most religious beliefs and values are the reason for their shame, guilt and anxiety.
       b.   Clients may discover that what they are doing is based on beliefs that are no longer functional.
       c.   Spiritual counseling encourages the client to turn their problems over to God and not take any action themselves.
       d.   Religious themes need to be addressed in every counseling session.

A-76   5. Ruth is counseling with a woman who describes an extremely unhappy marriage. Ruth suggests that she consider leaving her husband. The client has a deep spiritual conviction that marriage is for life and is not willing to consider divorce as an option. Ruth attempts to change her client's viewpoint as being unhealthy. In this case, Ruth is:

       a.   teaching her client to look at the negative consequences of her decision.
       b.   exploring the client's spiritual reasons for staying in the marriage.
       c.   imposing her values on the client instead of exploring the client's reasons for staying in the marriage.
       d.   helping her client to explore healthy options.

A-98   6. Thomas has full-blown AIDS and has decided to end his life rather than continue to suffer. The counselor he is working with does not condone rational suicide. In this case, the counselor needs to:

a. refer him to a competent professional qualified to assist the client.
b. learn as much as possible about the course of the client's illness.
c. explore the impact of the client's religious beliefs on making his decision to end his life.
d. help the client seek medical treatment that will help him cope with his pain.

C-97   7. According to the National Association of Social Workers policy on working with end-of-life decisions, it would NOT be appropriate for the professional to:

a. facilitate exploration of alternatives
b. help patients express their thoughts and feelings
c. deliver, supply, or personally participate in the commission of an act of assisted suicide
d. provide information to make an informed choice
e. deal with issues of grief and loss

F-95   8. The Death with Dignity Act is law in which state?

a. New York
b. Texas
c. Oregon
d. none of the above

C-95   9. All of the following are criteria to evaluate whether a person's suicide or hastened death is rational EXCEPT for which statement?

a. The person considering suicide has an unremitting and hopeless condition.
b. The person is unable to afford medical treatment.
c. The person is acting under his or her own free will.
d. The person is engaged in a sound decision-making process that includes consultation with a mental health professional.

C-87   10. Which of the following statements is most accurate?

a. Only about 33% of the U. S. population view religious faith as being a very important part of their lives.
b. Approximately 96% of psychologists believe religious faith is important in their own lives.
c. Counselors must understand their own spiritual/religious beliefs if they hope to gain an in-depth appreciation of the beliefs of their clients.
d. When clients are searching for meaning in life, it is appropriate for therapists to strongly suggest they seek religion as an answer.

CHAPTER 4 MULTICULTURAL PERSPECTIVES AND DIVERSITY ISSUES

C-111   1. The term *minority group* has come to refer to:

a. a sense of identity that stems from common ancestry, history, nationality, religion and race.
b. any relationship between two or more diverse groups.
c. any category of people who have been discriminated against or subjected to unequal treatment and oppression by society largely because of their group membership.
d. any pattern of behavior that denies access to opportunities or privileges to members of one racial group.

F-111   2. _____ counseling is any counseling relationship in which the counselor and the client belong to different cultural groups, hold different assumptions about social reality, and subscribes to different world views.

a. Culturally encapsulated
b. Diversity-sensitive
c. Multicultural
d. Transcultural

C-113   3. The culturally encapsulated counselor is characterized by:

    a.   defining reality according to the client's reality.
    b.   showing sensitivity to cultural variations among individuals.
    c.   evaluating other viewpoints and making attempts to accommodate the behavior of others.
    d.   defining reality according to one set of cultural assumptions.

C-113   4. A cross-cultural counselor who perceives reality exclusively through the filters of his or her own life experiences is said to be culturally:

    a.   immersed
    b.   ignorant
    c.   encapsulated
    d.   biased

C-120   5. Statements such as "Minority groups need to take responsibility for their own predicament" and "In order to succeed, people need to stop complaining and start working" do not take into account of environmental factors. These are examples of:

    a.   stereotypical beliefs.
    b.   guiding principles for action.
    c.   cultural tolerance.
    d.   challenging culture-bound values.

A-124   6. Frank is a Native American college student who is seeking information about his career choice from a male counselor. The counselor notices that he uses very little eye contact and needs to recognize that Frank:

    a.   lacks trust about the information he is receiving.
    b.   is unlikely to follow through with his suggestions.
    c.   is likely to view direct eye contact as a lack of respect.
    d.   would be more likely to have direct eye contact if the counselor were a female.

C-128   7. Marie is working with a lesbian client who is in a dysfunctional relationship with another woman. She is seeking counseling to sort out her options regarding leaving her emotionally abusive partner. Marie can assist her client by:

    a.   automatically attributing her client's problems to her sexual orientation.
    b.   attempting to change the sexual orientation of her client.
    c.   supporting her client's attempt to leave the abusive relationship, work on her abuse issues, and eventually enter into a positive lesbian relationship.
    d.   encouraging her client to realize how difficult it is to live in a lesbian relationship.

C-133   8. It is the authors' position that counselors would *not* work well with diverse populations if they:

    a.   are open to being challenged and tested.
    b.   are flexible in applying theories to specific situations.
    c.   believe that they are free from any racist attitudes, beliefs, and or feelings.
    d.   are comfortable with differences that exist between themselves and their clients.

A-134   9. Denise is an Euro-American social worker who is a former welfare client. She had four children when she was divorced and succeeded in completing her degree and getting off the system in four years. She is now working in a work-to-welfare program and sets similar goals for her multicultural clients. Denise's attitude and actions indicate that she:

    a.   believes in her client's ability to achieve and they will live up to her expectations.
    b.   is well intentioned and willing to challenge her clients.
    c.   can serve as a model of what her clients can accomplish with their lives--if she could do it, so could her clients.
    d.   is operating out of the majority value system and presuming that her clients want the same goals.

C-140   10. According to the authors, the first step in the process of acquiring multicultural counseling skills in a training program should be that students:

     a.   take a self-exploratory class to help identity their cultural and ethnic blind spots.
     b.   open themselves to people in other cultures through reading and travel.
     c.   free themselves from all racist thoughts, actions and feelings.
     d.   have their value system conform with an "acceptable norm".

CHAPTER 5 CLIENT RIGHTS AND COUNSELOR RESPONSIBILITIES

C-150   1. Informed consent generally implies that the person:

     a.   does not have the capacity to consent.
     b.   verbally gives consent.
     c.   has been persuaded or coerced to sign the consent form.
     d.   has the capacity to consent and has freely, without undue influence expressed consent.

F-150   2. _____ to give informed consent means that the client has the ability to make rational decisions.

     a.   Comprehension of information
     b.   Voluntariness
     c.   Capacity
     d.   Willingness

C-154   3. Written consent forms should NOT include:

     a.   a discussion of how a managed care system will affect the treatment, if applicable.
     b.   a detailed description of what will occur in therapy and a guarantee that the client will resolve their issues.
     c.   a statement describing the counselor's theoretical   orientation and how this will affect treatment.
     d.   clarification pertaining to fees and charges and procedures for filing for insurance reimbursement.

C-160   4. Henry is seeking counseling through his managed care provider. Ethically, he needs to be informed that a diagnosis:

     a.   can become a permanent part of his file.
     b.   of a severe emotional problem will exclude him from getting services.
     c.   is not required if he does not give his approval.
     d.   will in no way influence the course of his treatment.

C-160   5. Most ethical codes specify that therapist should:

     a.   be available to their clients even when they are on vacation.
     b.   inform clients that their records are inaccessible to them.
     c.   inform clients that a diagnosis can become a permanent part of their file and have ramifications in terms of cost of insurance, long-term insurability, and employment.
     d.   alter case notes that are damaging to the client if they are subpoenaed into court.

F-167   6. _____ should include a record of client and therapist behavior that is clinically relevant, including interventions used, client responses to treatment strategies, the evolving treatment plan, and any follow-up measures taken.

     a.   Assessments
     b.   Progress notes
     c.   Intakes
     d.   Screenings

C-169   7. Concerning counseling via the Internet, which statement is most accurate?

    a.   The codes of the major professional organizations offer detailed guidance regarding ethical practices in the use of technology.
    b.   There are both advantages and disadvantages in using Internet technology to deliver counseling services.
    c.   Most experts agree that what is being currently offered via Internet counseling is a form of traditional psychotherapy.
    d.   This form of counseling is not suited to a problem-solving approach.

C-174   8. Regarding counseling with children and adolescents, informed consent of parents or guardians may not be legally required when a minor is seeking counseling for:

    a.   dangerous drugs or narcotics.
    b.   sexually transmitted diseases.
    c.   pregnancy and birth control.
    d.   all of the above

A-177   9. Marie is a counselor who has been working with the parents of their six-year old daughter. They want Marie to counsel with their child since the effects of their stormy marriage is negatively affecting her behavior. Marie is hesitant to do so since she has no experience working with children. The ethical codes of most professional organizations would specify that:

    a.   she would have to use different types of therapy to work effectively with the child.
    b.   it would be unethical for Marie to counsel the child if she has not been trained in that area.
    c.   she needs to take specialized training in parent education before working with the child.
    d.   Child Protective Services need to be called.

C-179   10. The social policy of de-institutionalization, as it applies to mental-health practices, involves the "least restrictive alternative" which requires that:

    a.   voluntary commitment be sought only after less restrictive alternatives have failed.
    b.   professionals commit clients who are delusional.
    c.   practitioners protect themselves from liability by getting a lawyer.
    d.   treatment be no more harsh, hazardous, or intrusive than necessary to achieve therapeutic aims and protect clients and others from physical harm.

F-181   11. _____ is the failure to render professional services or to exercise the degree of skills that is ordinarily expected of other professionals in a similar situation.

    a.   Professional negligence
    b.   Ethical incompetence
    c.   Malpractice
    d.   Malfeasance

C-181   12. Malpractice is generally limited to incidents in which the practitioner:

    a.   used a procedure within the realm of accepted professional practice.
    b.   employed a technique that he or she was not trained to use.
    c.   used a procedure in which the client did not respond favorably.
    d.   explained the possible consequences of treatment and the client still wanted to participate in the process.

C-181   13. To succeed in a malpractice claim, the plaintiff needs to show that a breach of duty did exist in which:

    a.   the practitioner failed to foresee a client's intention to harm themselves even after a comprehensive risk assessment was made.
    b.   the client failed to get better in spite of reasonable care.
    c.   there was no professional relationship between therapist and client.
    d.   the practitioner failed to provide the appropriate standard of care.

C-182   14. _____ have received the greatest attention in the literature as grounds for malpractice suits.

    a. Violations of confidentiality and sexual misconduct
    b. Client abandonment and misdiagnosis
    c. Failure to obtain informed consent and practicing beyond the scope of competency
    d. Client abandonment and repressed or false memory

A-183   15. Joyce was hospitalized as a result of an attempted suicide. She has tried to call her therapist before taking an overdose of pills, but he could not be reached because he was on vacation and did not provide a substitute while he was gone. This action constitutes the following type of professional negligence:

    a. misdiagnosis
    b. client abandonment
    c. marked departure from established therapeutic practice
    d. practicing beyond the scope of competency

C-185   16. Inappropriate socialization with clients, burdening clients with a counselor's personal problems, and putting clients in awkward business situations are examples of:

    a. inappropriate crisis intervention.
    b. established therapeutic practices.
    c. mishandling of a client's transference or counselor's countertransference.
    d. seeking balance in the counseling relationship.

C-182   17. Which of the following is NOT listed as a reason for malpractice suits?

    a. failure to obtain or document informed consent
    b. practicing beyond the scope of competency
    c. unhealthy transference relationships
    d. engaging in a bartering arrangement with a client

C-187   18. The following is a safeguard against malpractice accusations:

    a. Give free sessions until the client is able to pay.
    b. Never engage in bartering under any circumstances.
    c. Avoid client's perception of abandonment by not taking time off.
    d. Practice in specific areas where you are competent.

C-190   19. In the event that a practitioner is sued he or she should:

    a. try to resolve the matter directly with the client.
    b. destroy or alter files or reports that may be incriminating.
    c. discuss the case with other professionals.
    d. promptly retain an attorney.

F-149   20. _____ can best be viewed as an ongoing process aimed at increasing the range of choices and the responsibility of the client as an active therapeutic partner.

    a. Diagnosis
    b. Informed consent
    c. Documentation
    d. Case consultations

CHAPTER 6 CONFIDENTIALITY: ETHICAL AND LEGAL ISSUES

C-196   1. The central right of clients concerning confidentiality is that:

    a. it guarantees that disclosures during therapy will be protected unless certain legal circumstances are present.
    b. everything said in therapy will always remain confidential.
    c. it is illegal to share information with anyone at anytime unless the client has signed an informed consent.
    d. their records cannot be subpoenaed into court.

A-198   2. James is in court facing drug-related charges and his therapist was subpoenaed to testify in court regarding any discriminating evidence concerning the case. His   therapist came to court but refused to answer questions regarding the case or produce James's records. The therapist used the following legal concept to protect himself from forced disclosure:

    a.   confidentiality.
    b.   privileged communication.
    c.   client privacy.
    d.   taking the 5th amendment.

F-199   3. _____ as a matter of law, refers to the constitutional right of an individual to decide the time, place, manner, and extent of sharing oneself with others.

    a.   Self-disclosure
    b.   Privileged communication
    c.   Privacy
    d.   Confidentiality

C-197   4. It is illegal and unethical for a therapist to disclose confidential information when:

    a.   the client consents to disclosure.
    b.   there is a duty to warn or to protect third parties.
    c.   an emergency exists.
    d.   an employer requests disclosure to determine the mental status of an employee without their consent.
    e.   there is a need to obtain appropriate consultations.

C-205   5. Ethical guidelines regarding confidentiality requires that counselors do NOT:

    a.   allow clerical assistants to handle confidential information.
    b.   use client records to consult with experts or peers.
    c.   use client case studies to teach or write books even when their clients' identities are disguised.
    d.   disclose client information unless there is clear and imminent danger to client or others or when legal requirements demand that confidential information be revealed.

A-209   6. Susan is quite distressed after finding out that her husband has been unfaithful and tells her counselor that she is so angry that she feels like killing him. In this case, the counselor needs to:

    a.   question Susan to determine whether she is likely to do physical harm to her husband.
    b.   warn the husband that he is in potential danger.
    c.   commit Susan to a hospital until she can overcome her anger.
    d.   warn Susan that she can be arrested for making threats against her husband.

C-210   7. The California court's ruling that requires that therapists breach confidentiality in cases where the general welfare and safety of others is involved is a result of the:

    a.   Bradley Center v. Wessner decision
    b.   Jablonski v. United States decision
    c.   Tarasoff decision
    d.   Hedlund v. Superior Court decision

A-212   8. A patient who was extremely upset over his wife's extramarital affair was voluntarily admitted to a psychiatric facility. After repeatedly threatening to kill both of them and admitting to his therapist that he had a weapon, he was given a weekend pass to visit his children who were living with his wife. He met his wife and lover at the house and killed both of them. The Bradley case illustrates the duty:

    a.   not to negligently release a dangerous client.
    b.   to involuntarily commit a dangerous client.
    c.   to breach client confidentiality under exceptional circumstances.
    d.   to warn anyone who is in the vicinity of the intended victim who might also be in danger.

C-213   9. _____ in a Supreme Court decision ruled that communications between licensed psychotherapists and their clients are privileged and therefore protected from forced disclosure in cases arising under federal law.

     a.   Bradley Center v. Wessner
     b.   Jablonski v. United States
     c.   Jaffee v. Redmond
     d.   Hedlund v. Superior Court

A-221   10. Jolene tells her counselor that she is depressed about the break-up of her relationship and "just wishes she could go to sleep and never wake up." In this case, the counselor needs to:

     a.   immediately commit Jolene to a psychiatric facility.
     b.   assess if Jolene is suicidal and intervene if necessary.
     c.   recognize that her statement is only a "cry for help" and should not be taken seriously.
     d.   see if there is any chance for reconciliation.

C-224   11. The following would be an ineffective way of managing a client's suicidal ideation:

     a.   Attempt to secure a promise from the client that he or she will not try to commit suicide.
     b.   Immediately hospitalize the client.
     c.   Be willing to communicate your caring without setting limits.
     d.   Recognize the limits of your competence and know when and how to refer.

C-224   12. Two processes that offer safeguards against malpractice liability in suicidal cases are:

     a.   consultation and documentation
     b.   assessment and orientation
     c.   intervention and hospitalization
     d.   diagnosis and informed consent

C-225   13. In regards to suicide, Szasz believes that mental-health professionals:

     a.   have an absolute professional duty to try to prevent suicide.
     b.   should support suicide prevention policies.
     c.   need to abstain from empowering agents of the state from using coercive means to prevent when an individual chooses to end their life.
     d.   need to document their client's suicide ideation.

C-210   14. According to the Tarasoff decision, the therapist does NOT:

     a.   need to accurately diagnose the client's tendency to behave in dangerous ways towards others before notifying authorities.
     b.   have a duty to warn the next of kin of suicidal patients.
     c.   have the right to break confidentiality even if the client is a threat to self or others.
     d.   need to be concerned about liability after notifying authorities of their clients threat to harm self or others.

C-228   15. Privileged communication does NOT apply in cases of:

     a.   clients' disclosures of personal and sensitive information.
     b.   child abuse and neglect.
     c.   unfaithfulness in one or both partners in couple's therapy.
     d.   legal proceedings where the therapist is asked to produce a client's records in court.

A-229   16. An African-American woman was interacting with her child in a domestic abuse shelter where she over-heard to say to her child "Keep touching that and I'm going to whoop you." The social worker who heard this statement should:

    a.   immediately report the mother to Child Protective Services.
    b.   tell the mother that she will be evicted from the shelter if she continues to talk to her child that way.
    c.   recognize that what constitutes abuse in one culture may not be viewed as abuse in another culture and not reportable until it is determined that the child is in danger.
    d.   remove the child from the mother's care until the mother can learn how to talk to her child with respect.

A-229   17. A single father reports that he had too much to drink and harshly spanked his three-year old son when he wouldn't stop screaming. The father feels terrible about the incident and asks his counselor to get some help for him so that it will never happen again. Acting on the highest level of ethical functioning, the counselor would:

    a.   place the child in foster care until the father can learn to deal more constructively with his anger.
    b.   consult with a colleague about referring her client to a treatment center.
    c.   examine all the factors and special circumstances of this case before acting.
    d.   immediately report the incident to Child Protection Services in order to protect the child.

C-236   18. A counselor working in an AIDS-related case:

    a.   has a legal duty to warn according to the Tarasoff decision.
    b.   is obliged to protect all third parties of the threat of HIV transmission according to ethical codes.
    c.   must report the case to the Department of Public Health.
    d.   has few legal guidelines to help them determine when or how to inform a potential victim of the threat of HIV transmission.

C-237   19. The following is a proposed ethical guideline for deciding when to disclose confidential information about a client's HIV status:

    a.   When there is suspicion that there is risk of harm to a third party.
    b.   When the third party is at risk of death or substantial bodily harm.
    c.   Third parties must be warned even where there is a state law that prohibits warning.
    d.   After there is an attempt to educate the client about high risk behavior.

C-239   20. In the case of disclosing confidential information when working with an HIV client, several writers state that therapist has a duty to protect when the following condition exists:

    a.   The client is engaging in safe-sex with a committed partner.
    b.   Clear and imminent danger must exist.
    c.   All potential victims must be warned, even if there have been multiple sexual partners over the years.
    d.   All persons who have exchanged needles with the client must be found and warned of possible danger.

CHAPTER 7 MANAGING BOUNDARIES AND MULTIPLE RELATIONSHIPS

A-246   1. Joe has a counseling practice and is also teaching psychology part-time at a university. He is well liked and trusted by students and some have asked for private counseling. Joe has decided to wait until semester break before taking them on as clients. Joe is:

    a.   exhibiting ethical behavior by telling his students that he will counsel them at the end of the semester.
    b.   in a dual relationship with his students which may cause ethical problems.
    c.   playing favoritism by not counseling all of his students.
    d.   not qualified to counsel his students because he is a part-time instructor.

C-247   2. The following is true concerning dual relationships:

a.   There is a clear consensus among practitioners regarding nonsexual relationships in counseling.
b.   Due to the fact that there are clinical, ethical, and legal risks, all blending of roles must be avoided.
c.   Objectivity in counseling is enhanced with dual relationships.
d.   Counselors need to make every effort to avoid dual relationships with clients that could impart professional judgment or increase the risk of harm to clients.

A-251   3. Ted is a counselor educator and also acts as therapeutic agent for his students' personal development since personal awareness is considered to be an intrinsic part of developing counselor skills in the program at the university in which he teaches. Ted is:

a.   totally unethical in attempting to guide his students towards self-awareness.
b.   involved in a situation in which he will become so subjective that he will be unable to teach his students.
c.   involved in role blending which is inevitable in the process of educating and supervising counselor trainees.
d.   in a situation that automatically leads to a conflict of interest.

F-250   4. Departures from commonly accepted practices that could potentially benefit clients are referred to as:

a.   unethical boundaries.
b.   boundary crossings.
c.   boundary violations.
d.   interpersonal boundaries.

C-251   5. The following action would maximize the risks inherent in dual or multiple relationships:

a.   Set healthy boundaries from the outset.
b.   Secure informed consent of clients and discuss with them both the potential risks and benefits of dual relationships.
c.   Document any dual relationships in clinical case notes.
d.   Become romantically involved with the client.

C-249   6. Linda is considering developing a multiple or dual relationship with her client and it's important for Linda to remember:

a.   that all multiple relationships should be avoided because they are usually harmful.
b.   that absolute answers are available to resolve dual or multiple relationship dilemmas.
c.   to be cautious in order to protect oneself from censure.
d.   to consider whether the potential benefit outweighs the potential for harm.

C-254   7. In regards to boundaries in the counseling relationship, Lazarus took the position that:

a.   certain ethics and boundaries actually diminish therapeutic effectiveness.
b.   all boundaries should be eliminated because they destroy the counseling relationship.
c.   strong boundaries must be maintained in order to avoid malpractice suits.
d.   traits such as flexibility, spontaneity, and warmth tend to be characteristics of therapists who maintain strong boundaries.

C-258   8. A professional entering into a bartering relationship, should do so only if:

a.   the client indicates that they don't have the funds to continue therapy.
b.   it involves an exchange of services.
c.   it does not involve a dual relationship.
d.   the relationship is not exploitative.

C-258   9. Therapist who are considering entering into a bartering arrangement would do well to consider all of the following recommendations EXCEPT:

a. Evaluate whether the bartering arrangement will put the therapist at risk of impaired professional judgment.
b. Determine the value of the goods or services in a collaborative fashion with the client at the onset of the bartering arrangement.
c. Allow the bartering arrangement to continue throughout the therapeutic relationship.
d. Document the bartering arrangement, including the value of good or services and a date on which the arrangement will end.

A-262   10. Marty is counseling with an Asian client who recently returned from a trip to Japan to visit relatives. His client wants to give him an inexpensive souvenir. It is important for Marty to:

a. refuse the gift on ethical grounds.
b. explain that the gift would change their relationship and create a conflict of interest.
c. be aware that accepting the gift is culturally appropriate with this client.
d. explain that he cannot accept the gift until the counseling relationship is over.

C-266   11. The counselor is likely to adopt stricter social boundaries and will be concerned about polluting the transference relationship if they are:

a. psychoanalytically oriented.
b. behavioral therapists.
c. working with culturally diverse clients.
d. already engaged in an active social life.

C-267   12. In a survey to study sexual attraction in the client-therapist relationship, it was determined
that:

a. most respondents reported never having been attracted to any client.
b. in most cases, sexual attraction was likely to lead to sexual relations.
c. fear of malpractice suits prohibited the therapist from acting out their attraction to clients.
d. most reported that even if they were attracted to a client, they refrained from having sexual relations with them.

C-267   13. A common reaction of therapists who realize that they have sexual feelings towards their clients is to:

a. feel anger at their own sexuality.
b. speak openly about the matter to the client.
c. investigate to see if the client feels the same.
d. feel guilty and fearful of losing control and being criticized.

C-268   14. Therapists can deal with powerful attractions to clients by:

a. repressing their feelings of attraction.
b. asking the client if the feeling is mutual.
c. terminating the relationship immediately.
d. monitoring boundaries by setting clear limits on physical contact, self-disclosure, and client requests for personal information.

C-276   15. Which one of the following is NOT considered a guideline to minimizing the likelihood of sexual transgressions by clinicians?

a. Seek professional support during times of personal loss or crisis.
b. Know the difference between sexual attraction to clients and acting out.
c. Avoid terminating the therapeutic relationship, even when sexual feelings obscure objectivity.
d. Monitor feelings and behaviors toward clients.

A-277   16. Bonnie became sexually involved with her therapist soon after therapy began. This action was initiated by the therapist who saw Bonnie's provocative behavior as an invitation to become intimate. The following is a possible on-going consequence for the client being sexually exploited:

   a.   substance abuse
   b.   suicidal ideation
   c.   distrust for therapists and the therapeutic process
   d.   impaired social adjustment and distrust of opposite sex
   e.   all of the above

C-278   17. Clients can file a legal complaint against a therapist for sexual misconduct by:

   a.   filing an ethical complaint with the therapist's professional association.
   b.   filing an ethical complaint with the therapist's licensing board.
   c.   lodging a complaint with the therapist's employer.
   d.   filing a criminal complaint or a civil suit.

C-273   18. According to professional codes of ethics, sexual relationships between client and counselor are considered to be ethical if:

   a.   the therapist is really in love with their client.
   b.   there is consent by the client.
   c.   they are not considered to be ethical under any circumstances.
   d.   the therapeutic relationship has ended and a referral has been given.

A-270   19. Robert is romantically attracted to his client and he suspects that the feeling is mutual. In order to take an ethical action, Robert should:

   a.   seek consultation with an experienced colleague, supervisor, or personal therapist who could help decide a course of action.
   b.   terminate therapy so they can develop a romantic   relationship.
   c.   repress his feelings and continue therapy with the   client.
   d.   explore his reasons for the attraction and tell the client why he was attracted to her.

C-284   20. In the author's view, non-erotic touching between counselor and client should be:

   a.   a spontaneous and honest expression of the therapist's feelings.
   b.   incongruent with what they feel.
   c.   a therapeutic technique used to extinguish catharsis.
   d.   considered unethical.

CHAPTER 8 PROFESSIONAL COMPETENCE AND TRAINING

C-295   1. The following statement would NOT be true in regards to professional codes of ethics in regards to counselor competence:

   a.   Practitioners are required to practice within the boundaries of their competence.
   b.   Only when the therapist completes a doctoral program, are they competent to practice with all specialties.
   c.   The practitioner can develop competency by working with professionals with more experience.
   d.   Conferences, workshops and continuing education are means towards developing competency.

C-302   2. According to the authors, a good training program encourages students to:

   a.   build on their life experiences and personal strengths and provides opportunities of expanding self-awareness.
   b.   emphasize skill training without consideration of personal development.
   c.   achieve a high enough GPA to pursue a doctorate.
   d.   specialize in one theory with the techniques and strategies that are unique to that theory.

A-299   3. James has applied to a counselor training program at a university. He is being oriented to the program according to ACA's guidelines which state that he would NOT need to be informed of the following:

a. The type and level of skill acquisition required for successful completion of the training.
b. The type of student and supervisee evaluation and dismissal policies and procedures.
c. Training components that encourage self-growth or self-disclosure as part of the training process.
d. The diversity of students applying to the program.

C-300   4. The argument for teaching a multimodal, systematic, technically eclectic model in training programs is that:

a. the variety of techniques and strategies taught can be applied to a wide range of problems with diverse clients.
b. it gives the student an opportunity to specialize in one theoretical approach.
c. there are few bureaucratic constraints when teaching this type of approach.
d. the student can learn to diagnose clients to fit the basic concepts of the theory being taught.

C-301   5. According to the authors, training programs need to be designed so that students can:

a. acquire a specialization that will keep them competitive in the job market.
b. place primary emphasis on acquiring and practicing skills that can be used for short-term therapy.
c. become generalists which will allow them to play a number of roles in various settings.
d. acquire a more thorough understanding of themselves as well as acquire theoretical knowledge.

F-308   6. _____ represents the least degree of regulation of professional practice.

a. Certification
b. Licensure
c. Registration
d. Accreditation

C-309   7. An argument put forth in favor of legislation to regulate the delivery of mental-health services is that:

a. professionalism builds up a rigid bureaucracy designed to protect the client.
b. the public is protected by setting minimum standards of service and holding professionals accountable.
c. there are as many certified charlatans as there are   uncertified, competent practitioners.
d. it contributes to professional specializations that pit one against the other.

C-310   8. Within the counseling profession, a specialty is officially recognized when:

a. practitioners achieve either a specialty accreditation through a group or certification through a professional organization.
b. the practitioner receives a doctorate degree.
c. the counselor works in a specific area for at least two years.
d. there is state regulation of the practice of that particular counseling specialization.

C-311   9. Most professional organizations support efforts to

a. require pro bono work at the rate of at least 20% of the work week for all professionals.
b. write regulations that encourage competition.
c. make continuing education a mandatory condition of relicensing.
d. require personality tests from all practitioners to ensure that those who enter the field are in good mental health.

F-314   10. _____ is an organized system by which practitioners within a profession assess one another's services.

    a.   Networking
    b.   Mentoring
    c.   Monitoring
    d.   Peer review

CHAPTER 9 ISSUES IN SUPERVISION AND CONSULTATION

C-327   1. In order to distinguish between the ethical and legal aspects of clinical supervision, the legal aspects involve:

    a.   supervisors' qualifications, along with their duties and responsibilities.
    b.   issues with dual relationships.
    c.   consent of trainees, clients, and third-party payers.
    d.   issues related to confidentiality, liability, the supervisor's duty to protect, and standards of care.

C-325   2. Supervisees in training programs do NOT have the right to:

    a.   be fully informed of their supervisor's approaches to supervision.
    b.   continual access to any records maintained during the supervisory relationship.
    c.   expect that the supervisor will be their personal therapist if needed.
    d.   confidentiality with regard to disclosure, unless mandated by law.

C-322   3. Supervisors are ethically vulnerable because:

    a.   there is a power differential between the participants.
    b.   of the "therapy like" quality of the supervisory relationship.
    c.   they are faced with protecting the welfare of clients, supervisees, the public and the profession.
    d.   all of the above.

C-321   4. It is NOT the responsibility of the supervisor to:

    a.   perform the role of teacher, counselor, or consultant as they are appropriate.
    b.   promote knowledge and skills required to effectively work with clients from culturally diverse backgrounds.
    c.   assist supervisees to recognize their personal limitations and protect the welfare of their clients.
    d.   independently decide the needs of the trainee, including the course of therapy they will need.

C-321   5. Which of the following statements in NOT accurate?

    a.   Supervisors or ultimately responsible, both ethically and legally, for the actions of their trainees.
    b.   Supervisors should not supervise more trainees than they can responsibly manage at one time.
    c.   Supervisors are not expected to maintain records pertaining to their work with supervisees.
    d.   It is essential that supervisors are familiar with the caseloads of their supervisees.

C-322   6. All of the following are ways in which supervisors can promote the personal and professional development of their supervisees EXCEPT for:

    a.   negotiating mutual decisions, rather than making unilateral decisions, about the needs of the trainee.
    b.   performing the role of teacher, counselor, or consultant when needed.
    c.   avoiding an evaluative role, lest the supervisee feel judged and develop performance anxiety.
    d.   assist supervisees in recognizing their personal limitations so as to protect the welfare of the clients.

A-322   7. Amy is in a counselor training program and has clients that she sees on a regular basis. Since she is a counselor trainee under supervision, Amy does NOT have to:

    a.   get informed consent from her client.
    b.   inform the client that she is a trainee.
    c.   be confidential with client information.
    d.   share client information with her supervisor.

C-331   8. Although the following is an important aspect of counseling it is NOT imperative that the trainee's supervisor:

    a.   have specialized training in methods of supervision.
    b.   have an in-depth knowledge of the specialty area in which they will provide supervision.
    c.   have professional certification in multicultural counseling theory and techniques.
    d.   provide timely and adequate supervision while monitoring and evaluating the supervisee's competence.

A-336   9. Susan is in a counselor training program and is infatuated with her supervisor. She has indicated that she is interested in pursuing an intimate relationship. In order to provide adequate supervision for Susan, her supervisor would need to:

    a.   clearly define and maintain ethical, professional, and social relationship boundaries with the student.
    b.   attempt to resolve the situation therapeutically.
    c.   suggest that she transfer to another training program.
    d.   let Susan know that there is no possibility for intimacy until she graduates from the program.

C-339   10. Professional codes of ethics for supervisors agree that:

    a.   social interaction with supervisees is essential to effective counselor training.
    b.   all dual or multiple relationships with supervisees are unethical.
    c.   sexual relationships between supervisors and students are unethical unless the student freely consents.
    d.   supervisors occupy a position of power and should not engage in sexual relationships with the student.

A-341   11. Martha is in a counselor training program and often discusses personal concerns with her supervisor. The purpose of this discussion is:

    a.   for the supervisor to initiate a therapeutic relationship with the trainee.
    b.   to facilitate the trainee's ability to work successfully with clients.
    c.   to resolve the trainee's problems so they work more effectively with clients.
    d.   to always make a referral to personal therapy.

A-344   12. Kenneth is involved in a specialized professional process which involves sharing expertise with others in the helping professions so they can better serve their own clients. He is functioning in the role of a:

    a.   therapist.
    b.   consultant.
    c.   supervisor.
    d.   broker.

C-345   13. The following is true concerning the process of consultation:

    a.   Consultation is a temporary process aimed at helping consultees move towards autonomy and independence.
    b.   Consultation is primarily aimed at dealing with personal problems rather than work concerns.
    c.   There are formal ethical guidelines specific to the   practice of consultation.
    d.   Consultees are obliged to follow the recommendations of the consultant.

C-346   14. A major professional issue for consultants is the degree to which their personal values will have an impact on their actions and decisions in the consultation process. It is critical that:

a.   difficult decisions be made for the consultees and support them with the follow-up action.
b.   the consultant investigate the goals of the organization to determine if they need to be changed.
c.   consultants present qualifications to show that they are competent to deliver the services being contracted.
d.   consultants make consultees aware that they may be providing services that are beyond their competency.

C-348   15. A good consultant contract:

a.   is general in nature until it can be determined what the problem is.
b.   leaves an open time frame until both parties are satisfied that the task has been accomplished.
c.   is a form of legal protection for both parties and can assist in developing clear understanding of the consultation process.
d.   allows the consultant to act in combination with the role of a counselor.

CHAPTER 10 ISSUES IN THEORY, PRACTICE, AND RESEARCH

C-357   1. Contemporary theories of counseling:

a.   are grounded on assumptions that are a part of Eastern culture.
b.   emphasize the uniqueness of the individual, self-assertion, and ego strength.
c.   focus on interdependence, and losing self in the totality of the cosmos.
d.   emphasizes the social and cultural facts of human existence.

F- 359   2. _____ is based on a negotiation between the client and therapist to define the therapeutic relationship including specifying the goals of therapy and methods likely to be used to obtain these goals.

a.   An agreement
b.   A contract
c.   A covenant
d.   A legally enforceable arrangement

C-361   3. When a counselor works in a managed care system, client's goals need to be:

a.   long-term and all encompassing.
b.   educational and therapeutic.
c.   geared towards the client gaining insight into his or her problems and movement towards self-actualization.
d.   highly specific, limited to reduction of problematic symptoms, and often aimed at teaching coping skills.

F-363   4. _____ is a general term covering the process of identifying an emotional or behavioral problem and making a statement about the current status of a client.

a.   Medical diagnosis
b.   Differential diagnosis
c.   Psychodiagnosis
d.   Individual diagnosis

C-364   5. Practitioners who argue *against* diagnosis:

a.   claim that DSM labels and stigmatizes people.
b.   are likely to be psychoanalytically oriented therapists.
c.   usually have a behavioristic orientation.
d.   are likely to work for a managed care system.

C-366   6. Therapists who fall into the category of clinicians who see diagnosis as being restrictive or who oppose diagnosis are likely to be:

    a.   directive therapists.
    b.   existential or relationship-oriented therapists.
    c.   psychoanalytic therapists.
    d.   those who practice from a multicultural framework.

C-366   7. The following is NOT true concerning therapeutic use of the DSM-IV to diagnose clients:

    a.   Emphasis is on pathology, deficits, limitations, problems, and symptoms.
    b.   It deals largely with culture-bound syndromes.
    c.   It is based on the assumption that distress in a family or social context is the result of individual pathology.
    d.   It is based on a systemic approach that views the source of distress as being within the entire system, rather than on the individual.

A-369   8. Mary is seeking counseling for relationship problems from her managed care facility. Her issues revolve around caretaking and the counselor is sure Mary can be helped through some assertiveness training. Since Mary does not fit into a DSM-IV category, the ethical therapist would most likely:

    a.   submit a claim using a DSM-IV category that is acceptable to the insurance company.
    b.   refuse to treat Mary because there may not be reimbursement for services rendered.
    c.   call the managed care company with a diagnosis so an appropriate treatment strategy can be recommended.
    d.   use a systems theory approach, and also submit an individual DSM diagnosis along with a comprehensive report detailing the impact of systems that affect Mary.

C-371   9. It would be appropriate to use the diagnostic category of "Dependent Personality Disorder" on:

    a.   Asian clients who tend to let their parents make important decisions for them.
    b.   a Native American client who quit his job to go back to the reservation because his parent was dying.
    c.   a Mexican-American client who is highly involved with her family even though she is married.
    d.   Caucasian college students who need to check with their parents before making any decisions, no matter how minor.

C-373   10. According to professional ethical principles on testing, it would be unethical for a counselor to:

    a.   perform testing and assessment services for which they have not been adequately trained.
    b.   develop, administer, score, interpret, or use assessment procedures that are appropriate for the situation.
    c.   test within the client's socialized behavioral or cognitive patterns.
    d.   consider the validity of a given test and interpret data in the context of the cultural characteristics of the client.

C-378   11. John is seeking counseling through his managed care provider and he needs to be informed that:

    a.   the managed care company may request the entire clinical record of a client.
    b.   he has the right to expect unlimited sessions.
    c.   his insurance provider will not have access to his records.
    d.   no referrals will be made upon termination of therapy.

C-376 12. The managed care model,

    a. allows practitioners to decide what clients need, how and when to treat them, and how long therapy will last.
    b. stresses time-limited interventions, cost-effective methods, and a focus on preventative strategies.
    c. has grown out of demands by practitioners for quality control and stabilizing escalating costs of mental-health care.
    d. encourages curative interventions, accurate diagnosis and hospital admissions when needed.
    e. assumes that practitioners will set therapeutic goals of personal growth and self-actualization for their clients.

C-382 13. Most who write about managed care seem to agree that the system is here to stay and that therapists will need to:

    a. open their own private practice to accommodate those who resist using their managed care resources.
    b. become trained or retrained in a body of knowledge and skills applicable to time-efficient and cost-effective therapies.
    c. concentrate on using psychoanalytic therapy with clients who need long-term care.
    d. avoid any family-of-origin issues when working with clients on a short-term basis.

C-377 14. What critical ethical issue(s) is(are) associated with managed care?

    a. informed consent
    b. confidentiality
    c. abandonment
    d. all of the above

C-382 15. Therapists cannot use the limitations of the managed care plan as a shield for failing to:

    a. render crisis intervention.
    b. make appropriate referrals.
    c. request additional services from the managed care plan.
    d. all of the above

CHAPTER 11 ETHICAL ISSUES IN COUPLES AND FAMILY THERAPY

C-396 1. The family systems perspective is grounded on the assumption that a client's problematic behavior may be:

    a. an individual problem that needs to be resolved before the family can meet in a group.
    b. the issue that is keeping the family in crisis.
    c. a symptom of dysfunctional patterns handed down across generations.
    d. a result of the individual's maladjustment and psychosocial development.

C-397 for: 2. All of the following are areas specifically addressed by the AAMFT Code of Ethics EXCEPT

    a. professional competence and integrity.
    b. giving gifts and receiving gifts from clients.
    c. responsibility to students and supervisees.
    d. responsibility to the profession.

C-398 3. According to couples and family ethical standards, the therapist needs to:

    a. focus the therapy on the identified patient.
    b. assure total confidentiality to family members who seek individual therapy sessions from the therapist.
    c. refrain from advertising their services.
    d. maintain high standards of professional competence and integrity.

C-401 4. According to the authors, the first order of importance of training family therapists is to:

    a.   acquire self-knowledge, especially with regard to family-of-origin issues.
    b.   learn basic counseling techniques to use with families and couples.
    c.   learn and practice specialties such as systems theory.
    d.   understand effective intervention techniques used when working with families and couples.

C-402 5. Gender sensitive models of training family therapists is aimed at:

    a.   raising consciousness concerning the role of cultural and ethnic factors in influencing the outlooks and behaviors of individuals and families.
    b.   overcoming trainee gender bias and sex-role stereo-typing.
    c.   understanding the collaborative nature of family therapy.
    d.   direct clinical contact with all members of the family system.

C-403 6. Most family therapy training programs employ both didactic and experiential methods and supervised practice. Experiential methods include:

    a.   classroom lectures, reading, and demonstrations.
    b.   both personal therapy and working with one's own family of origin.
    c.   films and videotapes of family therapy sessions.
    d.   role playing and discussion.

A-406 7. Natalie is a marital therapist who believes that marriage is a sacred institution and is dedicated to preserving marital relationships whenever possible. She is working with a couple who is attempting to resolve their problems even though they have also considered the possibility of divorce. One could expect that she:

    a.   would set her values aside and work with any decision that her clients chose to make about their marriage.
    b.   would place the primary focus on helping each person examine what is the best course of action for themselves.
    c.   might let it be known that she believes in the preservation of marriage and would urge the couple to work on their issues.
    d.   would consider divorce as a viable option if the couple is unhappy with their relationship.

C-408 8. Feminist family therapists are concerned about shifting the power balance between women and men in the family. Therefore, it is NOT likely that they would:

    a.   focus exclusively on the couple's relationship.
    b.   question gender-specific roles.
    c.   place the same demands for change on both women and men.
    d.   value the expression of emotion and nurturance in both men and women.
    e.

C-409 9. Below is a sex biased therapist response to problems presented in couples therapy:

    a.   Assuming that remaining married may not be the best choice for a woman.
    b.   Demonstrating equal interest in both the woman's career and the man's career.
    c.   Encouraging couples to accept the fact that child rearing is primarily the responsibility of the mother.
    d.   Shows some value bias whether or not the wife or husband had an affair.

C-413 10. The authors take the following position in regards to confidentiality in couples and family therapy:

    a.   "Hidden agenda" are seen as material that should be brought out into the open during a family session.
    b.   Therapists should not divulge in a family session any information given to them in an individual session.
    c.   Therapist need to inform clients that any information given during private sessions will be divulged in accordance with the greatest benefit to the family.
    d.   Family therapists are exempt from reporting information that could harm the family system.

CHAPTER 12 ETHICAL ISSUES IN GROUP WORK

C-422   1. The primary reason that therapy groups fit well into the managed care scene is because they:

      a.   can be designed to be brief and cost-effective treatments.
      b.   provide a sense of community to serve as an antidote to an impersonal culture in which many clients live.
      c.   serve the purpose of teaching interpersonal skills.
      d.   provide a natural laboratory that demonstrates to people that they are not alone and there is hope for creating a different life.

C-424   2. The current trend in training for group workers focuses on learning group process by:

      a.   didactic course work.
      b.   becoming involved in supervised experiences.
      c.   administering psychological tests to trainees.
      d.   all of the above

F-423   3. The Professional Training Standards of Group Workers specify:

      a.   a set of core knowledge.
      b.   skill competencies.
      c.   both knowledge and skill competencies.
      d.   specialized training for advanced group leadership.

C-424   4. The authors recommend at least three experiences as adjunct to a training program for group workers that would NOT include:

      a.   personal (private) psychotherapy.
      b.   experience in group therapy, group counseling, or a personal-growth group.
      c.   recognition that professional codes, legislative mandates, and institutional policies alone will ensure competent group leadership.
      d.   participation in a supervision and training group.

C-433   5. With respect to confidentiality, group leaders have a responsibility to:

      a.   clearly define what it means.
      b.   explain its importance.
      c.   inform members of the difficulties involved in enforcing it.
      d.   all of the above

C-436   6. Which of the following is NOT considered to be one of the characteristics of diversity sensitive group work?

      a.   Group counselors respect members' religious and spiritual beliefs and values.
      b.   Group counselors respect the roles of family and community hierarchies within a client's culture.
      c.   Group counselors treat all members the same.
      d.   Group counselors acquire the knowledge and skills necessary for working with diverse clients.

A-430   7. Gail feels like she has not accomplished what she wanted in her therapy group and has decided to leave. Gail's therapist needs to:

      a.   encourage her to explain why she wants to leave to other group members.
      b.   encourage her to leave before her negative attitude affects other members of the group.
      c.   put undue pressure on her to stay in group.
      d.   encourage other members to pressure her to stay.

C-431   8. The following is true in regards to group ethics:

     a.   As a rule, group leaders should conduct only those types of groups for which they have been trained.
     b.   The legal concept of privileged communication applies in group settings the same as it applies to individual sessions.
     c.   Group leaders are not obliged to inform psychiatric hospital patients that they are documenting group sessions.
     d.   Parents and guardians have the legal right to all communications that have occurred in groups for minors.

C-437   9. Below is an example of a technique being used in an unethical way:

     a.   modifying techniques so they are suitable for the client's cultural and ethnic background.
     b.   practicing unfamiliar techniques in group.
     c.   have a therapeutic purpose and be grounded in some theoretical framework.
     d.   members are given the freedom on whether or not they wish participate in a given experiment.

A-439   10. Andy is in a grief group and seems "stuck" in his sorrow over the death of his father. The leader realizes that Andy needs to work on this issue even though the group is coming to a close. He believes that Andy could best benefit by a technique that will allow him to openly express his emotions. In this case, the group leader should make an ethical decision to:

     a.   introduce the technique even though there is no chance to process after group.
     b.   recognize the potential adverse effects of techniques used to elicit emotions and take precautions to ensure that there is time to process.
     c.   persuade Andy to participate in the technique even if he seems reluctant, since it is essential to express grief openly.
     d.   make sure Andy has a good support system so he won't feel abandoned when group terminates.

CHAPTER 13 ETHICAL ISSUES IN COMMUNITY WORK

F-449   1. _____ are attempts to change the social environment to meet the needs of he population as a whole and are carried out by influencing social policy.

     a.   Direct community services
     b.   Indirect community services
     c.   Community organization services
     d.   Community counseling services

F-449   2. Direct client services focuses on:

     a.   outreach activities.
     b.   client advocacy.
     c.   consultation.
     d.   influencing policymakers.

C-451   3. Counselors who work in the community need to recognize that it would be an error to:

     a.   use community resources as a way to enrich therapy.
     b.   believe that one person or group has a monopoly on the helping process.
     c.   work with client problems in their cultural context.
     d.   attend to the network of the client's support systems.

A-451   4. Nakita is an African-American mother with four children and has been having trouble finding housing in a safe community. Lisa is her social worker and suspects that there may be racial discrimination involved and takes her to sites that she has previously screened for availability. In this case, Lisa is acting as an:

     a.   evaluator.
     b.   adviser.
     c.   advocate.
     d.   ombudsman.

C-451   5. In this role, counselors assist clients in recognizing oppressive forces in the community as a source of their problem and teach their clients strategies for developing political power to bring about change in the clients' social and physical environment:

   a.   change agent
   b.   consultant
   c.   adviser
   d.   advocate

C-452   6. Counselors can encourage ethnic minority clients to learn skills they can use to interact successfully with various forces in their community by acting as their

   a.   advocate.
   b.   broker.
   c.   adviser.
   d.   consultant.

A-452   7. Tony is a recently relocated Mexican-American who is seeking help from a Spanish-speaking organization designed to meet the needs of newly arriving legal immigrants. Tony is quite depressed, but reluctant to talk to his counselor about his problems. The counselor refers him to an indigenous resource who is more likely to be trusted by Tony. He was referred to:

   a.   a paraprofessional worker.
   b.   either a folk or spiritual healer from the community.
   c.   an intern from a counseling program.
   d.   a community organizer.

A-452   8. Chong is a legal immigrant and is having post-traumatic stress symptoms as a result of his experiences in Laos. He may be reluctant to use the available counseling recourses because he:

   a.   harbors the attitude that he should be able to take charge of his own life.
   b.   may perceive the resources as culturally insensitive.
   c.   believes that it is only for people who have extreme symptoms.
   d.   all of the above

C-459   9. Lay volunteers from the community receive thirty hours of training before working in the abuse shelter. They receive supervision at the site and are considered to be:

   a.   indigenous workers.
   b.   nonlicensed workers.
   c.   counseling professionals.
   d.   professional community service worker.

C-463.   10. Many professionals struggle with the issue of how to work within a system while retaining their dignity, vitality, and convictions. The most important component in any effort to bring about change is to:

   a.   make an honest self-examination to determine the degree in which the "system" is actually hindering them.
   b.   start the process of changing the system by speaking to the director of the organization.
   c.   conduct research as to the reasons for the problems in the organization.
   d.   evaluate the options in responding to unacceptable circumstances.

Answer Key for
CHAPTER QUIZZES for Issues and Ethics in the Helping Professions, Sixth Edition

CHAPTER 1	CHAPTER 5	5. d	3. d
1. c	1. d	6. d	4. c
2. d	2. c	7. a	5. a
3. b	3. b	8. d	6. b
4. c	4. a	9. c	7. d
5. a	5. c	10. c	8. d
6. d	6. b	11. a	9. d
7. b	7. b	12. d	10. a
8. c	8. d	13. d	11. a
9. a	9. b	14. d	12. b
10. b	10. d	15. c	13. b
	11. c	16. e	14. d
CHAPTER 2	12. b	17. d	15. d
1. c	13. d	18. c	
2. a	14. a	19. a	CHAPTER 11
3. a	15. b	20. a	1. c
4. a	16. c		2. b
5. c	17. d	CHAPTER 8	3. d
6. c	18. d	1. b	4. a
7. c	19. d	2. a	5. b
8. b	20. b	3. d	6. b
9. d		4. a	7. c
10. b	CHAPTER 6	5. d	8. a
	1. a	6. c	9. c
CHAPTER 3	2. b	7. b	10. c
1. a	3. c	8. a	
2. c	4. d	9. c	CHAPTER 12
3. b	5. d	10. d	1. a
4. b	6. a		2. b
5. c	7. c	CHAPTER 9	3. c
6. a	8. a	1. d	4. c
7. c	9. c	2. c	5. d
8. c	10. b	3. d	6. c
9. b	11. c	4. d	7. a
10. c	12. a	5. c	8. a
	13. c	6. c	9. b
CHAPTER 4	14. b	7. d	10. b
1. c	15. b	8. c	
2. c	16. c	9. a	CHAPTER 13
3. d	17. c	10. d	1. b
4. c	18. d	11. b	2. a
5. a	19. b	12. b	3. b
6. c	20. b	13. a	4. c
7. c		14. c	5. a
8. c	CHAPTER 7	15. c	6. d
9. d	1. b		7. b
10. a	2. d	CHAPTER 10	8. d
	3. c	1. b	9. b
	4. b	2. b	10. a

PART 5

**PRACTICE EXAMINATION for
Issues and Ethics in the Helping
Professions, Sixth Edition**

Directions: These true-false examination questions are based upon the textbook, **Issues and Ethics in the Helping Professions, Sixth Edition.** The intent of this practice examination is to serve as a comprehension check for your level of mastery of the reading. By taking this test, and using it as a tool for review, you will likely improve your performance on the final examination for the course. In taking the exam, decide if the statement is more true or more false. Some of the items are subject to interpretation, and the answers could vary depending on one's perspective. In the case of this type of statement or question, use the authors' perspective given in the textbook. (At times, the question includes the qualifier "According to the authors. . .")

1. Law and ethics are basically synonymous concepts.

2. Community standards (or mores) are universal, in that they apply to all mental-health disciplines, to all theories, and to all geographical areas.

3. Principle ethics typically focuses on acts and choices.

4. According to the authors, most violations of ethics probably happen quite inadvertently in counseling practice.

5. Because most ethical violations are readily detected, ethical codes are easy to enforce.

6. Ethical codes are partially designed to protect practitioners against charges of malpractice, for counselors who conscientiously practice in accordance with these codes have some measure of defense in case of legal action.

7. The ethical codes of the professional organizations provide ready-made answers to ethical dilemmas that practitioners face.

8. Virtue ethics asks "Am I doing what is best for my client?"

9. The principle of nonmaleficence refers to applying the maximum professional skill and competence for promoting the growth and development of clients.

10. The principle of autonomy refers to therapists making efforts at fostering maximum self-development on the part of clients.

11. The principle of fidelity refers to providing equal treatment to all people regardless of age, sex, race, ethnicity, disability, socio-economic status, cultural background, religion, or sexual orientation.

12. The principle of veracity means that practitioners are truthful with their clients.

13. The feminist model of ethical decision making calls for client involvement in the process of making such decisions.

14. Therapists often report that burnout resulted from the nonreciprocated giving and the responsibility demanded by the therapeutic relationship.

15. Transference is sometimes referred to as the "unreal" relationship in therapy.

16. It is both possible and desirable for counselors to be scrupulously neutral with respect to values in the counseling relationship.

17. Counselors often give clients clues about their values through their nonverbal and body messages.

18. The authors contend that counselors who impose their values (in indirect ways) on their clients are behaving unethically.

19. According to the authors, counselors would do well to state their own values in cases involving value conflicts between therapist and client.

20. Ethically, counselors should refer a client if they have not struggled with exactly the same value issue.

21. In any case where counselors do not agree with the value systems of their clients, ethical practice dictates that they refer these clients to another professional.

22. According to the authors, there is no place in counseling for discussing religious or spiritual values, as this type of discussion is best done with a minister, priest, or rabbi.

23. The authors believe that clients' values should be respected, but challenged by the therapist.

24. The authors contend that values should be kept out of therapy.

25. Informed consent is especially important when working under a managed care system.

26. Giving clients access to their files seems to be consistent with the consumer-rights movement.

27. The practice of involuntary commitment of people to mental institutions raises difficult professional, ethical, and legal issues.

28. In order for clients to develop trust in their therapist, it is essential that they know that confidentiality will not be compromised under any conditions.

29. Legally, there are three elements to adequate informed consent: autonomy, good will, and empathy.

30. The process of educating clients about their rights might well begin with having them sign informed-consent documents.

31. Confidentiality should be considered as an absolute.

32. At the outset, clients have a right to know about the benefits and the risks involved in psychological treatment.

33. One of the major obstacles to the open sharing of files with clients is the need to give clients a diagnostic classification as a requirement for receiving third-party reimbursements.

34. The ethical responsibility of counselors to safeguard clients from unauthorized disclosures of information given in the therapy relationship is the definition of privileged communication.

35. In privileged communication, the waiver belongs to the therapist.

36. When it is necessary to break confidentiality, it is not a good policy to invite the client to participate in this process.

37. Clients in a managed care program should be informed that confidentiality may be compromised under this system.

38. Generally speaking, the legal concept of privileged communication does not apply to group counseling.

39. Most of the ethical codes contain guidelines for safeguarding a client's right to privacy.

40. Therapists have both an ethical and a legal responsibility to clarify the limitations of confidentiality.

41. It is generally agreed that therapists do not have a duty to protect suicidal clients, if these clients decide that they want to take their own life.

42. The Jaffee case resulted in an extension of privileged communication for licensed psychotherapists.

43. The Hedlund case held that the therapist must accurately diagnose the client's condition for behaving in dangerous ways toward others.

44. The Jablonski case ruled that the protective privilege ends where the public peril begins.

45. It is expected that the decision in the Jaffee case will have far-reaching consequences for licensed psychotherapists and their clients.

46. Civil liability means that an individual can be sued for not doing right or for doing wrong to another.

47. Perhaps the best way to protect yourself from a malpractice suit is to restrict your practice to clients for whom you are prepared by virtue of your education, training, and experience.

48. Malpractice is more of an ethical concept than a legal concept.

49. To prevent their being sued, practitioners are expected to possess and exercise the knowledge, skill, and judgment common to other members of their profession.

50. Violations of confidentiality and sexual misconduct have received the greatest attention in the literature as grounds for malpractice suits.

51. In the counseling relationship dual/multiple relationships are always unethical.

52. According to the authors, counselors who establish any form of social relationships with former clients are necessarily engaging in unethical practice.

53. Counselors who become aware of sexual attractions to their clients can be sure that they are involved in countertransference.

54. Touching that does not lead to intercourse is associated with older and more experienced therapists.

55. The practice of bartering therapy for either goods or services is generally considered to be both unethical and illegal.

56. In those cases when there is the potential for negative consequences arising from a dual relationship, it is the practitioner s responsibility to consult with other professionals or seek supervision.

57. Therapist sexual involvement with clients is both unethical and illegal.

58. Concerning sexual intimacy between therapist and client, most professional organizations do not have a specific code condemning this practice.

59. Increasingly, clients are successfully suing therapists who engaged in sex with them.

60. Most codes of ethics specify that sexual intimacy with a former client is considered unethical before two years after termination.

61. Specialization training applies to all levels of education, from associate of arts to doctoral programs.

62. Most licenses specify the types of clients or problems the licensee is competent to work with, as well as specifying the techniques a practitioner is competent to use.

63. A major problem of the peer-review process is the difficulty in determining the qualifications of the reviewers.

64. Licensure is the most inclusive, legislatively established basis of credentiality.

65. The process of certification and licensure can be the basis for professional jealousy over turf and can lead to restrictive regulation that is motivated by competition for access to the marketplace.

66. It is considered appropriate for supervisors to provide therapy for their supervisees when they have personal problems that affect their clients.

67. Counselors are often expected to function in the roles of both supervisor and consultant.

68. Supervisors are ultimately responsible, both ethically and legally, for the actions of their trainees.

69. Trainees do not have a legal or an ethical right to periodic feedback and evaluation from their supervisor.

70. Supervisors have a legal and ethical obligation to respect the confidentiality of client communications.

71. Sexual intimacies between a supervisor and a supervisee should not be considered unethical if both parties consent.

72. The topic of competence in supervision is incomplete without taking into consideration the role of cultural factors in the supervisory relationship and the competence of supervisors in this area.

73. Supervisors themselves need supervision if they hope to enhance their own multicultural development.

74. Before initiating a contract, consultants should investigate the goals of the organization to determine whether they can support them.

75. Dual/multiple relationships do not apply in cases of consulting.

76. In using tests with minority clients, it is important to proceed with caution if the instrument was not standardized by including minority populations.

77. In order to create a meaningful research design to evaluate the outcomes of psychotherapy, it is not necessary to obtain informed consent of the clients.

78. Practitioners with a psychoanalytic orientation tend not to favor psychodiagnosis.

79. Some writers have noted that cultural factors are often neglected in both research and theory.

80. Issues in theory, practice, and research are necessarily separate and distinct.

81. Most of the ethical codes mention the practitioner's responsibility for recognizing the special needs of diverse client populations.

82. Failure to address cultural factors in counseling relationships often constitutes unethical practice.

83. Multiculturalism has been referred to as the "third force" in counseling.

84. Regardless of one's cultural background, silence in a counseling session can always be seen as a form of resistance.

85. There is a great deal of scientific evidence that supports the position that minority clients should always be treated by minority therapists.

86. Cultural tunnel vision, or cultural encapsulation, can result in unethical behavior in multicultural counseling situations.

87. It is a good policy to provide children with treatment alternatives and enlist their participation in defining goals for their therapy.

88. Most states now require specialized training in gender-sensitive therapy as a condition for relicensure.

89. In most states specialized training in counseling gay and lesbian clients is required for relicensure.

90. Virtually all states have mandatory reporting laws in cases of child abuse or suspected child abuse.

91. In child custody cases, confidentiality is limited when therapists are called on to give expert testimony.

92. At this time, there are no ethical guidelines specific to the practice of marital and family therapy.

93. From a legal perspective, members in a group generally waive privileged communication, since a third party is present.

94. There are virtually no psychological risks involved in participating in a group.

95. People have a right to know what they are getting into before they make a commitment to become a part of any group.

96. Group leaders who have not participated in their own individual and group therapy are guilty of unethical practice.

97. The community counselor focuses primarily on the person-in-the-environment.

98. Counselors working from a community perspective examine dysfunctional behavior by focusing on the dynamics within the client that have led to the client's personal problems.

99. Outreach strategies are particularly important in reaching ethnic minorities.

100. For many ethnically diverse clients, seeking help in the form of traditional counseling is foreign.

Answer Key for
Practice Examination for Issues and Ethics in the Helping Professions, Sixth Edition

1.	F	26.	T	51.	F	76.	T
2.	F	27.	T	52.	F	77.	T
3.	T	28.	F	53.	F	78.	F
4.	T	29.	F	54.	T	79.	T
5.	F	30.	T	55.	F	80.	F
6.	T	31.	F	56.	T	81.	T
7.	F	32.	T	57.	T	82.	T
8.	T	33.	T	58.	F	83.	F
9.	F	34.	F	59.	T	84.	F
10.	T	35.	F	60.	T	85.	F
11.	F	36.	F	61.	T	86.	T
12.	T	37.	T	62.	F	87.	T
13.	T	38.	T	63.	T	88.	T
14.	T	39.	T	64.	T	89.	F
15.	T	40.	T	65.	T	90.	T
16.	F	41.	F	66.	F	91.	T
17.	T	42.	T	67.	T	92.	F
18.	T	43.	F	68.	T	93.	T
19.	T	44.	F	69.	F	94.	F
20.	F	45.	T	70.	T	95.	T
21.	F	46.	T	71.	F	96.	F
22.	F	47.	T	72.	T	97.	T
23.	T	48.	F	73.	T	98.	F
24.	F	49.	T	74.	T	99.	T
25.	T	50.	T	75.	F	100.	T

PART 6

**FINAL EXAMINATION for
Issues and Ethics in the Helping
Professions, Sixth Edition [2003]**

Directions Please use SCANTRON [Form 884] and a number 2 pencil. Leave no blanks on your answer sheet and make only one response per item. Select the one best answer. BE SURE TO RECORD THIS TEST NUMBER ON YOUR SCANTRON SHEET AND RETURN THIS TEST WITH YOUR ANSWER SHEET TO THE INSTRUCTOR DIRECTLY.

MULTIPLE CHOICE QUESTIONS
Below are 200 multiple choice items. Decide on the ONE BEST response. Leave no blanks and erase clearly and make no stray marks. Note: Some of the test items might be subject to interpretation. In these cases, consider the perspective given by the authors of the textbook.

CHAPTER 1 INTRODUCTION TO PROFESSIONAL ETHICS

1. Ethical issues in the mental health professions are regulated:
   a. by legislation.
   b. by professional codes.
   c. both by legislation and professional codes.

2. Law and ethics:
   a. are two distinct entities.
   b. share common elements.
   c. are synonymous.

3. The first level of ethical functioning is characterized by compliance with the law and by following: the ethical codes. This is called
   a. personal ethics.
   b. ideal ethics.
   c. aspirational ethics.
   d. mandatory ethics.
   e. basic ethics.

4. A higher level of ethical functioning is sometimes known as
   a. personal ethics.
   b. ideal ethics.
   c. aspirational ethics.
   d. mandatory ethics.
   e. basic ethics.

5. All are a limitation of professional codes of ethics EXCEPT for which of the following?
   a. Conflicts sometimes emerge within ethics codes as well as among various organizations' codes.
   b. Ethics codes are designed more to protect professionals than to protect clients.
   c. Ethics codes tend to be proactive rather than reactive.
   d. Some issues cannot be handled by ethical codes alone.

6. Which of the following statements is NOT correct?
   a. Codes are intended to be a blueprint that would remove the need for the use of judgment and ethical reasoning.
   b. Ethical codes tend to be conservative by nature.
   c. Codes were developed to protect the profession from outside regulation, and thus they reflect what most professionals can agree on.
   d. Final authority must rest with the practitioners in making decisions.
   e. Ethical codes need to be understood within a cultural framework, and therefore they must be adapted to specific cultures.

7. Community standards:
   a. may serve as the legal criteria for determining whether a practitioner provided an acceptable standard of care.
   b. always dictate the development of ethical codes.
   c. are the only basis for making sound ethical decisions.
   d. are more rigorous than ethical standards.
   e. are essentially the same thing as ethical standards.

8. Principle ethics:
   a. focuses on the use of rational, objective, universal, and impartial principles in the analysis of ethical dilemmas.
   b. focuses on the character traits of the counselor.
   c. asks the question "Am doing what is best for my client?"
   d. is the highest level of ethical standards expected of a counselor.

9. Virtue ethics asks which of the following questions?
   a. Is what I am doing legal?
   b. Is this situation unethical?
   c. Am I doing what is best for my client?
   d. Is there a basic conflict between the ethical and legal course?
   e. How can I best protect myself from a malpractice suit?

10. The following principle implies avoidance of doing harm, which includes refraining from actions that risk hurting clients:
    a. autonomy.
    b. beneficence.
    c. nonmaleficence.
    d. justice, or fairness.
    e. veracity.

11. This principle refers to therapists making efforts at fostering maximum self-determination on the part of clients:
    a. autonomy.
    b. beneficence.
    c. nonmaleficence.
    d. justice, or fairness.
    e. fidelity.

12. This principle refers to providing equal treatment to all clients, regardless of age, sex, race, ethnicity, disability, cultural background, religion, or lifestyle:
    a. autonomy.
    b. beneficence.
    c. nonmaleficence.
    d. justice, or fairness.
    e. fidelity.

13. This principle refers to applying the maximum professional skill and competence for promoting the growth and development of clients:
    a. autonomy.
    b. beneficence.
    c. nonmaleficence.
    d. justice, or fairness.
    e. veracity.

14. Of the following steps in making an ethical decision, which one step would most likely be the *initial step* taken by a practitioner in resolving an ethical dilemma?
    a. Enumerate the consequences of various decisions.
    b. Consider possible and probable courses of action.
    c. Obtain consultation.
    d. Identify the problem, or dilemma.
    e. Review the relevant ethical guidelines.

15. Which of the following would be the *last step* when making an ethical decision?
    a. Obtain consultation.
    b. Decide on what appears to be the best course of action.
    c. Enumerate the consequences of various decisions.
    d. Identify the potential issues involved.
    e. Check with an attorney to prevent a malpractice suit.

CHAPTER 2 THE COUNSELOR AS A PERSON AND AS A PROFESSIONAL

16. Concerning the issue of unresolved personal conflicts, the authors take the position that:
    a. the personal needs of a therapist can interfere with the therapeutic process if the therapist is unaware of these needs.
    b. therapists must resolve all their personal difficulties before they begin to counsel others.
    c. counselors must have experienced exactly the same problems as their clients in order to have empathy for their clients.
    d. none of the above

17. What would NOT be a good rationale for therapy for the therapist?
    a. Those who counsel others should know what the experience of being a client is like.
    b. Therapy can assist the helper in becoming aware of his needs and motivations.
    c. Therapy can clarify our values as they apply to the therapy process.
    d. In order to be an effective therapist, he or she must be free of blind spots and resolve all his or her unfinished business.

18. Transference is sometimes referred to as the "unreal" relationship in therapy. This implies that:
    a. transference is merely a figment in the client's imagination.
    b. clients project onto their therapists past feelings or attitudes they had toward significant people in their lives.
    c. therapy is an artificial relationship.
    d. transference is not an important issue in therapy.

19. Studies on stressful client behaviors for therapists have shown which of the following to be most stressful?
    a. apathy or lack of motivation
    b. not believing in the value of therapy
    c. premature termination
    d. suicidal statements

20. Countertransference is best considered as:
    a. feelings of genuine concern of the therapist for clients.
    b. the client's projections toward the therapist.
    c. any projections by a therapist that can potentially get in the way of helping a client.
    d. empathy demonstrated by the therapist for the client.
    e. normal feelings of therapists toward clients.

21. Countertransference becomes an ethical issue when the:
    a. client's needs assume priority over the therapist's needs.
    b. counselor's unresolved conflicts get in the way of effective therapy.
    c. client uses session time to work through his or her problems.
    d. client puts all the blame for their difficulties on the therapist.

22. Which of the following is NOT listed as a form of countertransference?
    a. development of sexual or romantic feelings
    b. being overprotective with clients
    c. the need for constant reinforcement and approval
    d. having genuine empathy for clients
    e. compulsive advice giving

23. In studies of therapists, which of the following was reported as the most stressful source of client behavior for therapists?
    a. clients' premature termination
    b. suicidal statements
    c. apathy or lack of motivation
    d. anger toward the therapist
    e. agitated anxiety

24. Delaying the termination of a client by a therapist can be considered:
    a. an attempt to help clients work through stubborn resistances.
    b. a form of fostering client dependence.
    c. a form of transference on the client's part.
    d. a measure of preventing malpractice suits.
    e. a legal requirement to provide a standard of care to the client.

25. Stress of mental-health professionals is primarily related to:
    a. events that occur in the therapist's work.
    b. irrational or unrealistic beliefs that many therapists hold.
    c. failure to have experienced their own therapy.
    d. the motivation of their clients to cooperate with therapy.

26. Professionals who are NOT at a high risk of burnout include:
    a. those who get most of their personal needs met through their social life outside of work.
    b. those who assume *unreasonable* responsibility for client outcomes.
    c. those who limit their work to one type of activity.
    d. those who work with very demanding clients.

27. The most common characteristic of the impaired practitioner is:
    a. empathy.
    b. denial.
    c. a high level of self-esteem.
    d. the willingness to offer pro bono services for clients who cannot afford therapy.
    e. a satisfactory level of intimacy in his or her own life.

28. Impaired counselors:
    a. have the ability to resolve stressful events.
    b. are able to function professionally.
    c. experience deterioration of therapeutic skills.
    d. are able to alleviate the suffering of their clients .

29. Which of the following statements is true about the impaired professional?
    a. Many counselors have avoided or denied the existence of the impairment issue.
    b. Much is known about the impact of impairment on clients.
    c. There is extensive research on counselor impairment.
    d. There are many professionally sponsored avenues to helping impaired professionals.

30. From the authors' perspective, what should students in a counseling program be told about the profession they are about to enter?
    a. Counseling can be a hazardous profession.
    b. Because practitioners use their own life experiences in their work, they are vulnerable to reexperiencing old wounds.
    c. There are stresses both from the nature of therapeutic work and from role expectations of therapists.
    d. Working with clients can open up the therapist's own issues.
    e. all of the above

CHAPTER 3 VALUES AND THE HELPING RELATIONSHIP

31. To the question "Is it possible for counselors to keep their values out of their counseling sessions?" the authors take the position that
    a. it is possible for counselors to be neutral with respect to values in the counseling relationship.
    b. it is desirable for counselors to be value neutral.
    c. it is neither possible nor desirable for counselors to be neutral with respect to values in the counseling relationship.
    d. counselors should keep their values hidden so that they won't contaminate their clients' choices.
    e. it is the counselors' job to influence their clients to adopt proper values.

32. Imposing of the counselor's values on a client is:
   a. illegal.
   b. generally considered unethical.
   c. both illegal and unethical.
   d. necessary when the client's values are in conflict with the counselor's values.

33. Counselors can influence their clients' values by:
   a. paying attention and reinforcing certain aspects of what their clients disclose.
   b. their nonverbal behavior.
   c. asking leading questions.
   d. all of the above

34. Ethically, counselors should refer a client when they:
   a. have sharp value conflicts with clients.
   b. are likely to persuade their clients to adopt a particular point of view.
   c. have not struggled with exactly the same value issue.
   d. do not experience warmth towards their clients.

35. Regarding the issue of differences in life experiences, the authors take the position that counselors need NOT:
   a. have a personal connection with their clients unless they have had similar life experiences.
   b. to be sensitive to the differences in their backgrounds.
   c. have experienced each of the struggles of their clients to be effective in working with them.
   d. be concerned with past life experiences since they are working in the here-and-now.

36. According to the National Association of Social Workers policy on working with end-of-life decisions, it would NOT be appropriate for the professional to:
   a. facilitate exploration of alternatives.
   b. help patients express their thoughts and feelings.
   c. deliver, supply, or personally participate in the commission of an act of assisted suicide.
   d. provide information to make an informed choice.
   e. deal with issues of grief and loss.

37. The Death with Dignity Act is law in which state?
   a. New York
   b. Texas
   c. Oregon
   d. Michigan

38. A way to minimize significantly the ethically questionable conversion of others to your values is to:
   a. inform yourself about the varieties of values held in society.
   b. be aware of your own values.
   c. present value options in an unbiased manner.
   d. respect clients who have values different from yours.
   e. all of the above

39. Most writers in the chapter on values tend to agree on which following principle?
   a. Therapists have the ultimate task of deciding what is best for their clients.
   b. Therapists have a role in promoting self-determination as a value for clients.
   c. If therapists have value differences with their clients, they should do what they can to convert their clients toward their own values.
   d. Under no circumstances is it appropriate for therapists to disclose their values to their clients, lest they sway them.

40. From the perspective of the authors, what is NOT role of values in therapy?
   a. Values are a crucial part of the therapy process.
   b. Clients' values should never be challenged by the therapist.
   c. Therapists need to consider why the client is seeking therapy.
   d. Values influence the direction of therapy.

CHAPTER 4 MULTICULTURAL PERSPECTIVES AND DIVERSITY ISSUES

41. Essential components of multicultural counseling include all of the following EXCEPT:
    a. counselors are aware of culture-specific methods of helping.
    b. counselors feel comfortable with their client's differing beliefs.
    c. counselors avoid becoming involved in out-of-office interventions.
    d. counselors are aware of how their own biases could affect minority clients.
    e. counselors can send and receive both verbal and nonverbal messages appropriately.

42. Which of the following is NOT one of the trends toward multicultural awareness?
    a. There is an increasing recognition of the universality and applicability of Western values for all cultures.
    b. There is a trend toward acquiring knowledge of culturally different clients and gaining experience in working with minority clients.
    c. There is a concern for adapting techniques and interventions in ways that are relevant for the culturally different client.
    d. There is recognition that counselor self-awareness is as important as cultural awareness in multicultural counseling situations.

43. A sense of identity that stems from common ancestry, nationality, religion, and race is defined as:
    a. culture.
    b. ethnicity.
    c. minority group.
    d. multicultural.
    e. ethnic-sensitive practice.

44. The generic term that refers to many different cultural environments in a pluralistic society, along with the relevant theories and techniques in counseling practice, is defined as:
    a. culture.
    b. ethnicity.
    c. minority group.
    d. multicultural.
    e. diversity-sensitive practice.

45. A category of people who have typically been discriminated against or subjected to unequal treatment is defined as:
    a. culture.
    b. ethnicity.
    c. minority group.
    d. multicultural.
    e. ethnic-sensitive practice.

46. A broad definition that can be associated with a racial or ethnic group as well as with gender, religion, economic status, nationality, physical capacity or handicap, or sexual orientation is the term:
    a. culture.
    b. ethnicity.
    c. minority group.
    d. multicultural.
    e. ethnic-sensitive practice.

47. The term "cultural encapsulation" implies:
    a. a multicultural awareness important for counseling practice.
    b. a level of hostility against values of minority groups.
    c. stereotypical thinking and ignoring of cultural differences.
    d. respect for the multiplicity of cultural values in our pluralistic society.

48. Western culture places prime value on all but which one of the following?
   a. choice
   b. emphasis on the patriarchal nuclear family
   c. measurable and visible accomplishments
   d. deference to the elderly and to authority figures
   e. getting things done and keeping busy

49. Statements such as "Failure to change stems from a lack of motivation" and "People have choices, and it is up to them to change their lives," do not take into account environmental factors. These are examples of:
   a. guiding principles for action in the diversity movement.
   b. stereotypic beliefs.
   c. cultural tolerance.
   d. challenges to culture-bound values.
   e. existential realities of living.

50. According to the authors, the first step in the process of acquiring multicultural counseling skills in a training program is that students:
   a. free themselves of all racists thoughts, feelings, and actions.
   b. take a self-exploratory class or workshop to help identify their cultural and ethnic blind spots.
   c. have their values systems conform with the majority culture.
   d. conduct research in attitudes pertaining to multicultural counseling.

51. For therapists who may work with lesbian, gay, and bisexual people it is their responsibility to:

   a. understand the special concerns of these individuals.
   b. develop the knowledge and skills to competently deliver services to these clients.
   c. become aware of their assumptions and attitudes toward sexual orientation.
   d. confront their own personal prejudices, myths, fears, and stereotypes regarding sexual orientation.
   e. all of the above

52. Which belief/attitude is NOT characteristic of the culturally skilled counselor?
   a. They can appreciate diverse cultures, and they feel comfortable with cultural differences.
   b. They are aware of their own values, attitudes, and biases and how they are likely to affect minority clients.
   c. They are committed to the importance of persuading their clients to accept the values of the dominant society.
   d. They are willing to refer a client because of their limitations in cross-cultural counseling.

53. Which of the following knowledge is NOT characteristic of the culturally skilled counselor?
   a. They are aware of institutional barriers that prevent minorities from using psychological services.
   b. They know all the diagnostic categories of DSM-IV as they apply to various minority groups.
   c. They understand the impact of oppression and racist concepts on the mental-health professions.
   d. They possess specific knowledge about the traditions and values of the group they are working with.

54. Which of the following skills is NOT characteristic of the culturally skilled counselor?
   a. They understand that one counseling style can be used equally effectively with all minority groups.
   b. They are able to send and receive both verbal and nonverbal messages accurately and appropriately.
   c. They are able to make out-of-office interventions when necessary by assuming the role of consultant and agent for change.
   d. They are able to employ institutional intervention skills on behalf of their clients.

55. The ethics codes of ACA, APA, and NASW clearly state that discrimination is unethical and unacceptable on the basis of all but which of the following?
   a. race
   b. ethnicity
   c. the counselor's level of education and training
   d. gender
   e. sexual orientation

CHAPTER 5 CLIENT RIGHTS AND COUNSELOR RESPONSIBILITIES

56. Most of the codes of ethics state that informed consent is required:
    a. only for voluntary clients.
    b. only for involuntary clients.
    c. only for adults.
    d. as a prerequisite for most forms of assessment and treatment.

57. The ethics codes specify that informed consent:
    a. is best completed at the initial meeting with a client.
    b. is accomplished before the client comes in for the initial session.
    c. begins when counseling is initiated and continues throughout the counseling process as necessary.
    d. is done only when the client requests it.
    e. is best initiated after several counseling sessions.

58. Which of the following is NOT a necessary legal element for adequate informed consent?
    a. autonomy
    b. capacity
    c. comprehension of information
    d. voluntariness

59. Informed consent procedures should have all but which of the following?
    a. costs
    b. a precise definition of every technique that may be used in therapy
    c. the length of therapy
    d. background of the therapist
    e. alternatives to traditional therapy

60. Student counselors generally meet regularly with their supervisors and fellow students to discuss their progress in any problems they encounter in their work. This practice:
    a. is unethical, but not illegal.
    b. shows that a counselor is technically incompetent.
    c. is a good policy for counselors to inform their clients that this is likely to occur.
    d. violates the client's confidentiality.

61. Giving clients access to their files:
    a. seems to be consistent with the consumer-rights movement.
    b. is an invitation to a malpractice suit.
    c. is legally, professionally, and ethically inappropriate.
    d. is generally unethical, but not generally illegal.
    e. should be done routinely for seriously disturbed clients.

62. Concerning counseling via the Internet, which statement is most accurate?
    a. The codes of the major professional organizations offer detailed guidance regarding ethical practices in the use of technology.
    b. There are both advantages and disadvantages in using Internet technology to deliver counseling services.
    c. Most experts agree that what is being currently offered via Internet counseling is a form of traditional psychotherapy.
    d. This form of counseling is not suited to a problem-solving approach.

63. Regarding counseling with children and adolescents, informed consent of parents or guardians may not be legally required when a minor is seeking counseling for:
    a. dangerous drugs or narcotics.
    b. sexually transmitted diseases.
    c. pregnancy and birth control.
    d. all of the above

64. Educating clients about the treatment process might well include exploring:
   a. what services the therapist will provide.
   b. how long the will treatment last.
   c. the behavior expected of the client.
   d. what financial considerations need to be taken into account.
   e. all of the above

65. For a practitioner who works under a managed care system, clients have a right to know that:
   a. they will have access to needed care that extends beyond their benefits.
   b. financial incentives exist to keep the amount or type of service limited.
   c. the number of sessions that are allowed will be determined by the type of therapy needed by the client.
   d. the system will have no access to their records.

66. If tape recording or videotaping of sessions is done, ethical practice dictates that;
   a. clients have a right to be informed about this procedure at the initial session.
   b. clients understand why and how these recording will be used.
   c. secret recordings will not be made.
   d. who will have access to the tapes.
   e. all of the above

67. Which of the following is an alternative to traditional therapy?
   a. peer self-help groups
   b. behavior therapy
   c. group therapy
   d. psychodynamic therapy

68. Proponents of using therapeutic contracts emphasize the:
   a. collaborative partnership of client and therapist.
   b. need for therapists to employ manipulation to uproot client defenses.
   c. value of keeping the therapeutic process mysterious.
   d. value of therapists promoting client dependence.
   e. the need to keep clients passive during the therapy process.

69. Regarding giving clients information about the possible benefits and risks of a treatment program, it is a good idea to:
   a. avoid talking about these issues too early in therapy, lest clients become needlessly anxious.
   b. give clients promises of specific outcomes, if they cooperate with the program.
   c. emphasize the role of client responsibility for outcomes.
   d. avoid talking about risks, but play up the benefits of therapy.

70. Which of the following would least likely be a part of the content of the informed consent process?
   a. background of the therapist
   b. testimonials from prior clients
   c. the length of therapy and termination
   d. the fact that consultation may occur with colleagues
   e. interruptions in therapy

71. The *main* purpose for maintaining client records is for:
   a. reimbursement by an insurance carrier.
   b. the protection of a therapist against a lawsuit.
   c. the benefit of the client.
   d. conducting research on the process and outcome of therapy.
   e. meeting the requirements of managed care policies.

72. Practitioners have an obligation to keep records for how long after a client terminates?
   a. one year
   b. four years
   c. seven years
   d. twenty years
   e. as long as the client is alive

73. Therapists who work with children and adolescents must:
   a. often function as advocates for their under-age clients.
   b. know the laws of their state.
   c. struggle with dealing with confidentiality issues.
   d. be willing to seek consultation in difficult ethical and legal situations.
   e. all of the above

74. What can a therapist do to avoid malpractice suits?
   a. use some form of a diagnostic system
   b. maintain prudent and reasonable practices in working with clients
   c. make use of informed consent
   d. keep adequate clinical records, documenting key aspects of therapy
   e. all of the above

75. One of the *best* ways to protect yourself from a malpractice suit is to:
   a. restrict your practice to clients for whom you are prepared by virtue of your education, training, and experience.
   b. insist that your clients sign a contract at the outset of therapy.
   c. tape record the counseling sessions.
   d. carry professional liability insurance.
   e. keep detailed notes.

76. Which condition is NOT essential for malpractice litigation?
   a. The therapist must have a duty to the client.
   b. The therapist must act in a negligent or improper manner.
   c. There must be a causal relationship between that negligence and the damage claimed by the client.
   d. The therapist must have engaged in illegal behavior.

77. Of the following which is the *major* cause of malpractice suits against mental-health professionals?
   a. misrepresenting one's professional training and skills
   b. the failure to keep adequate records
   c. accepting gifts from clients
   d. sexual misconduct
   e. faulty diagnosis

78. Therapists cannot protect themselves from malpractice suits when they:
   a. don't keep records so their notes or observations cannot be used against them in court.
   b. clearly define issues pertaining to fees at the outset of therapy.
   c. consult with colleagues when they are in doubt.
   d. refuse to accept gifts from your clients.
   e. make use of informed-consent procedures.

79. In case you are involved in a malpractice suit, what should you do?
   a. Destroy or alter any files that could incriminate you.
   b. Discuss the case with as many people as possible to get ideas of what to do next.
   c. Seek out the client who is suing you and attempt to change his or her mind.
   d. Seek consultation with an attorney.
   e. Continue the professional relationship with the client who is suing you, lest you be charged with abandonment.

80. Which of the following is NOT a trend in legal liability?
   a. Malpractice suits will be more effective against those therapeutic approaches that are highly directive and active.
   b. Family therapy will prompt suits by family members who are dissatisfied with the outcomes.
   c. Private practitioners are less vulnerable to litigation than they were in the past.
   d. There will be an increase in the use of informed-consent doctrine in cases of negligence.
   e. There will be an increase in suits over approaches that have not been effective as short-term therapies.

CHAPTER 6 CONFIDENTIALITY: ETHICAL AND LEGAL ISSUES

81. The legal right which exists by statute and which protects the client from having his confidences revealed publicly from the witness stand during legal proceedings without his or her permission is the definition of:
    a. confidentiality.
    b. privileged communication.
    c. privacy.
    d. informed consent.

82. The ethical responsibility of mental-health professionals to safeguard clients from unauthorized disclosures of information given in the therapeutic relationship is the definition of:
    a. confidentiality.
    b. privileged communication.
    c. privacy.
    d. informed consent.

83. The freedom of individuals to choose for themselves the time, place, manner, and extent of sharing oneself with others is the definition of:
    a. confidentiality.
    b. privileged communication.
    c. privacy.
    d. informed consent.

84. In privileged communication,:
    a. the waiver belongs to the therapist.
    b. the waiver belongs to the client.
    c. the waiver belongs to either the therapist or client, depending on the case involved.
    d. the therapist has the right to invoke the privilege against the client's wishes.

85. Since the therapist/client privilege is a legal concept, which of the following is a circumstance in which information must be provided by the therapist?
    a. when the therapist is acting in a court-appointed capacity
    b. when the client initiates a lawsuit against the therapist
    c. when the therapist determines that the client is in need of hospitalization
    d. all of the above

86. When it becomes necessary to break confidentiality,:
    a. it is wise to try to keep this from the client so as not to arouse suspicion and negatively affect the relationship.
    b. it is a good practice to inform the client of the intention to take this action.
    c. it is unwise to invite the client to participate in this process.
    d. the therapist should refer the client to another professional.
    e. the therapist should reveal the maximum amount of information possible.

87. Which of the following is NOT one of the legal trends in confidentiality?
    a. There are ethical grounds for the safeguarding of confidentiality.
    b. Confidentiality can be absolutely ensured under a legal framework.
    c. How counselors carry out this professional obligation is increasingly being specified by law.
    d. The therapeutic process seems to proceed adequately without the existence of absolute confidentiality.

88. Which of the following statements is NOT true as it relates to the issue of confidentiality?
    a. The counselor has a responsibility to explain the degree of confidentiality they can promise.
    b. It is seen as ethical to break confidentiality when child abuse is suspected, but it is not a legal requirement in most states.
    c. Confidentiality cannot be considered an absolute.
    d. Accepted ethical standards do not clearly define circumstances when confidentiality should be broken.
    e. Confidentiality must be broken in cases where the client is a danger to themselves and others.

89. Legally, confidentiality must be broken:
    a. when an employers requests records.
    b. when an insurance company is paying for treatment.
    c. if records are subpoenaed into court.
    d. when the client is a threat to self or others.

90. The responsibility to protect the public from dangerous acts of violent clients entails liability for civil damages when practitioners neglect this duty by:
    a. failing to diagnose or predict dangerous behavior.
    b. failing to warn potential victims of violent behavior.
    c. failing to commit dangerous individuals.
    d. prematurely discharging dangerous clients from the hospital.
    e. all of the above

91. Which case dealt with the duty NOT to negligently release a dangerous patient?
    a. the Tarasoff case
    b. the Bradley case
    c. the Jablonski case
    d. the Hedlund case
    e. the Jaffee case

92. Which case dealt with the decision holding that the therapist must accurately diagnose the client's condition for behaving in dangerous ways toward others, and so not allow negligent release?
    a. the Tarasoff case
    b. the Bradley case
    c. the Jablonski case
    d. the Hedlund case
    e. the Jaffee case

93. The following guiding principle was the basis for the decision in which court case? "The public policy favoring protection of the confidential character of patient-psychotherapist communications must yield to the extent to which disclosure is essential to avert danger to others. The protective privilege ends where the public peril begins."
    a. the Tarasoff case
    b. the Bradley case
    c. the Jablonski case
    d. the Hedlund case
    e. the Jaffee case

94. The duty to warn not only the potential victim, but also anyone who might be near the intended victim, and who might also be in danger, was affirmed by the:
    a. Tarasoff case.
    b. Bradley case.
    c. Jablonski case.
    d. Hedlund case.
    e. Jaffee case.

95. Which case underscores the duty to commit a dangerous individual and therapist's negligence for failure to commit?
    a. the Tarasoff case
    b. the Bradley case
    c. the Jablonski case
    d. the Hedlund case
    e. the Jaffee case

96. Which case represented a victory for mental health organizations, since it extended the confidentiality privilege for licensed psychotherapists?
    a. the Tarasoff case
    b. the Bradley case
    c. the Jablonski case
    d. the Hedlund case
    e. the Jaffee case

97. Which of the following is NOT one of the characteristics associated with suicide-prone behavior?
    a. The suicide rate for women is about three times greater than that of men.
    b. Up to 80% of suicides were preceded by a prior attempt.
    c. Feelings of hopelessness and depression tend to be associated with suicidal intentions.
    d. A definitive plan of action is an indicator.
    e. Unemployment increases the risk for suicide.

98. Who has developed a case arguing that mental health professionals do NOT have an absolute duty to prevent suicide?
    a. Jourard
    b. Glasser
    c. Szasz
    d. Rogers
    e. Wubbolding

99. Under the case for suicide prevention which of the following is *false*?
    a. Once a counselor determines that a significant risk does exist, appropriate action must be taken.
    b. Failure to take action can result in the therapist's being held liable.
    c. Consider decreasing the frequency of the counseling sessions, so as not to create dependency on the client.
    d. Develop a therapeutic contract with suicidal clients.
    e. Do not make yourself the only person responsible for the decisions and actions of your client.

100. Which of the following is NOT advisable when working with a suicidal client?
    a. increasing the frequency of counseling sessions
    b. labeling the client as suicidal
    c. encouraging the client to call you in times of crisis
    d. bringing significant others into the client's social network, with his or her permission
    e. considering the use of medication

CHAPTER 7 MANAGING BOUNDARIES AND MULTIPLE RELATIONSHIPS

101. What is an accepted ethical guideline in terms of having social and personal relationships with clients?
    a. Therapists are advised to avoid dual relationships with their clients.
    b. Friendships with clients always have positive results in counseling.
    c. Counseling a friend is beneficial to both people involved.
    d. Any form of social relationships with clients always damages the therapeutic relationship.
    e. These dual relationships are not only highly unprofessional and unethical, but also illegal in most states.

102. The practice of bartering psychotherapy for either goods or services:
    a. is considered unethical by virtually all the ethical codes.
    b. has the potential for conflicts.
    c. is generally an illegal practice.
    d. is always an attempt of the therapist to control the client.
    e. presents no problems if both the therapist and the client agree on bartering arrangements.

103. Which of the following is an example of a relationship that involves blending of roles, yet with clear beneficial potential?
    a. sex in the supervisory relationship
    b. forming friendships with former clients
    c. bartering
    d. mentoring
    e. combining business ventures with therapy relationships

104. When there is potential for negative consequences arising from a dual relationship, it is the responsibility of the professional to:
    a. secure the informed consent of clients and discuss with them both the potential risks and benefits of the relationship.
    b. consult with other professionals.
    c. seek supervision if the risk for harm is high.
    d. document any dual relationships in clinical case notes.
    e. all of the above

105. Dual/multiple relationships are generally prohibited because:
   a. these relationships are also illegal.
   b. such relationships always impair professional judgment.
   c. there is a danger of exploiting the client.
   d. clients often misuse their power in the transference relationship.
   e. these relationships always entail a conflict of interest.

106. Concerning ethical standards on sexual intimacy in therapy,:
   a. virtually all of the professional organizations now have a specific statement condemning sexual intimacies in the client/therapist relationship.
   b. only the APA has specifically included sexual intimacy with clients as unethical.
   c. most professional organizations do NOT have a specific code condemning sexual intimacies in therapy.
   d. none of the existing codes have any definite procedures for filing and processing ethical complaints against therapists.

107. The rationale for the conviction that sexual relationships between a therapist and client is both unethical and professionally inappropriate is that:
   a. doing so involves the abuse of the power that therapists have by virtue of their function and role.
   b. it fosters dependency on the client's part.
   c. the objectivity of the therapist is lost.
   d. clients are usually psychologically hurt by such practices.
   e. all of the above

108. The legal sanctions against therapists who engaged in sex with their clients include:
   a. being sued for malpractice.
   b. not being able to continue one's professional practice.
   c. having their licenses revoked or suspended by the state.
   d. being ordered to undergo therapy to resolve their own problems.
   e. all of the above

109. Concerning nonerotic physical contact with clients, therapists of which orientation tend to make most use of this practice?
   a. behavior-modification
   b. rational-cognitive
   c. humanistic
   d. psychodynamic
   e. systemic

110. If you become aware of unethical behavior on the part of a colleague, most codes of ethics state that:
   a. the matter must be reported to the ethics committee immediately.
   b. it is best to discuss the matter with the colleague.
   c. there is a need to ignore the situation, because taking any action may only make matters worse.
   d. it is mandatory to write a report describing the details of the unethical behavior in case of a lawsuit.

111. A professional entering into a bartering relationship, should do so only if:
   a. the client indicates that they don't have the funds to continue therapy.
   b. it involves an exchange of services.
   c. it does not involve a dual relationship.
   d. the relationship is not exploitative.

112. Marty is counseling with an Asian client who recently returned from a trip to Japan to visit relatives. His client wants to give him an inexpensive souvenir. It is important for Marty to
   a. refuse the gift on ethical grounds.
   b. explain that the gift would change their relationship and create a conflict of interest.
   c. be aware that accepting the gift is culturally appropriate with this client.
   d. explain that he cannot accept the gift until the counseling relationship is over.

113. The counselor is likely to adopt stricter social boundaries and will be concerned about polluting the transference relationship if they are:
    a. psychoanalytically oriented.
    b. behavioral therapists.
    c. working with culturally diverse clients.
    d. already engaged in an active social life.

114. A common reaction of therapists who realize that they have sexual feelings towards their clients is to:
    a. feel anger at their own sexuality.
    b. speak openly about the matter to the client.
    c. investigate to see if the client feels the same.
    d. feel guilty and fearful of losing control and being criticized.

115. According to the authors, non-erotic touching between counselor and client should be:
    a. viewed as clinically inappropriate.
    b. generally avoided because of potential lawsuits.
    c. a spontaneous and honest expression of the therapist's feelings.
    d. avoided because of the potential for this to become sexual.

CHAPTER 8 PROFESSIONAL COMPETENCE AND TRAINING

116. Concerning making referrals, therapists have an ethical responsibility:
    a. to refer a client if they feel at all uncomfortable in the relationship.
    b. to refer clients to other professionals when working with them is beyond their professional training.
    c. to refer a clients if they have not experienced the client's problem.
    d. all of the above

117. Which of the following actions is inappropriate when a counselor thinks that he or she is unqualified to work with a particular client?
    a. avoid initiating the counseling relationship
    b. terminate the relationship
    c. suggest appropriate alternatives
    d. provide a referral
    e. continue to counsel the client if he or she does not want a referral

118. Counseling programs can be held legally liable for counselors who graduated from their program and:
    a. prove to be incompetent.
    b. are involved in dual relationships with their clients.
    c. received good grades, yet were in therapy to deal with some personal problems.
    d. practiced as a specialist in an area that they were not trained in.

119. According to the authors, a good training program encourages students to
    a. build on their life experiences and personal strengths and provides opportunities of expanding self-awareness.
    b. emphasize skill training without consideration of personal development.
    c. achieve a high enough GPA to pursue a doctorate.
    d. specialize in one theory with the techniques and strategies that are unique to that theory.

120. Training programs need to be designed so that students can acquire:
    a. a more thorough understanding of themselves.
    b. theoretical knowledge.
    c. a range of skills they can apply to diverse client populations.
    d. all of the above
    e. none of the above

121. According to the authors, one of the best ways to teach students how to effectively relate to a wide range of clients is:
    a. through formal lectures.
    b. to present specialized techniques in working with various client groups.
    c. for faculty to model healthy interpersonal behavior.
    d. for students to engage in research on treatment strategies.

122. Training programs have a responsibility to:
    a. honor their commitment to the students they admit.
    b. protect future consumers who will be served by those who graduate.
    c. both of the above
    d. none of the above

123. Most professional organizations support efforts to:
    a. require pro bono work at the rate of at least 20% of the work week for all professionals.
    b. write regulations that encourage competition.
    c. make continuing education a mandatory condition of relicensing.
    d. require personality tests from all practitioners to ensure that those who enter the field are in good mental health.

124. Licensure assures the public that the licensee:
    a. has undergone their own personal therapy.
    b. has completed maximum education and training.
    c. is thoroughly competent to practice in areas they advertise.
    d. has met certain specific requirements in terms of education and training.

125. Most licenses:
    a. are generic in nature.
    b. specify the types of clients or problems the licensee is competent to work with.
    c. specify the techniques a practitioner is competent to use.
    d. ensure that practitioners will competently do what their licenses permit them to do.
    e. all of the above

126. Licenses and certifications:
    a. are designed to protect consumers.
    b. require applicants to be in personal therapy.
    c. generally rely on faculty recommendations to determine which applicant has met the standards of competence.
    d. are required only for therapists who have acquired a specialization

127. All of the following are arguments for licensing, EXCEPT for which one?
    a. The welfare of the consumer is better protected with the legal regulation than without it.
    b. Licensing allows the profession to define for itself what it will do and will not do.
    c. Licensing is designed to protect the public from ignorance about mental-health services.
    d. Licensing decreases the chances that practitioners' services will be better distributed.
    e. Licensing upgrades the profession.

128. A weak point of mandatory continuing education is that:
    a. legally professional organizations cannot require practitioners to acquire necessary hours.
    b. professional organizations cannot require practitioners to be intellectually and emotionally involved in continuing education.
    c. professional organizations cannot monitor the quantity and quality of continuing education activities.
    d. it is impossible for organizations to specify approved continuing education activity as a basis for recertification.

129. A drawback of the peer review model is implied in which question?
    a. Will professionals volunteer as peer reviewers?
    b. Are peers able to competently be involved in a review process?
    c. Who determines the quality of the peer reviewer?
    d. Can peers be objective?

130. Which of the following is NOT true about continuing education?
    a. It is mandatory in every state when seeking relicensure.
    b. It keeps practitioners up to date with new research and knowledge in their area of specialty.
    c. It helps to sharpen one's counseling skills.
    d. Many professional organizations require it for recertification.
    e. Gaining professional competence is an on-going process.

CHAPTER 9 ISSUES IN SUPERVISION AND CONSULTATION

131. Which one of the following is NOT the responsibility of a clinical supervisor?
    a. Supervisors are responsible for the actions of their trainees.
    b. Supervisors must check on the trainees' progress and be familiar with their caseloads.
    c. Supervisors must inform trainees about the goals and process of supervision.
    d. Supervisors must be willing to provide personal therapy to trainees when trainees have personal problems that affect their clients.

132. Legally, clinical trainees are NOT required to make their clients aware that
    a. they are trainees.
    b. they meet regularly for supervision sessions.
    c. their cases may be discussed in group supervision meetings.
    d. their grade depends on their success with the client.

133. Supervisors who have sexual contact with trainees are:
    a. engaging in dual relationships.
    b. opening themselves to legal liability for failure to provide adequate supervision.
    c. exploiting their power as supervisors.
    d. in violation of the codes of ethics.
    e. all of the above

134. In the case of counselor educators who counsel their students, this practice is:
    a. always unethical.
    b. illegal in most states.
    c. always the decision of the counselor educator and the student involved.
    d. specifically mentioned in most of the ethical codes.

135. Under what circumstances should a therapist consult with colleagues or specialists?
    a. when a client complains of physical symptoms
    b. when facing an ethical problem
    c. when working with a client for an extended period of time and losing objectivity
    d. when there are apparent conflicts between legal and ethical aspects
    e. all of the above

136. The authors believe that the most important element in the supervisory process is the supervisor's ability to:
    a. teach methods and techniques that are up-to-date.
    b. establish an effective collaborative working relationship with supervisees.
    c. use a directive style of supervision.
    d. be an effective therapist for their trainees.

137. Supervisors in counseling training programs bear both direct liability and vicarious liability. Vicarious liability pertains to:
    a. derelict supervision of trainees.
    b. inappropriate advice given to trainees about treatment.
    c. responsibilities that supervisors have because of the actions of their trainees.
    d. giving tasks to trainees that exceed their competence.

138. In order to distinguish between the ethical and legal aspects of clinical supervision, the legal aspects involve:
    a. supervisors' qualifications, along with their duties and responsibilities.
    b. issues with dual relationships.
    c. consent of trainees, clients, and third-party payers.
    d. issues related to confidentiality, liability, the supervisor's duty to protect, and standards of care.

139. Supervisees in training programs do NOT have the right to:
    a. be fully informed of their supervisor's approaches to supervision.
    b. continual access to any records maintained during the supervisory relationship.
    c. expect that the supervisor will be their personal therapist if needed.
    d. confidentiality with regard to disclosure, unless mandated by law.

140. Supervisors are ethically vulnerable because:
    a. there is a power differential between the participants.
    b. of the "therapy like" quality of the supervisory relationship.
    c. they are faced with protecting the welfare of clients, supervisees, the public and the profession.
    d. all of the above
    e. none of the above

141. It is NOT the responsibility of the supervisor to:
    a. perform the role of teacher, counselor, or consultant as they are appropriate.
    b. promote knowledge and skills required to effectively work with clients from culturally diverse backgrounds.
    c. assist supervisees to recognize their personal limitations and protect the welfare of their clients.
    d. independently decide the needs of the trainee, including the course of therapy they will need.

142. Although the following is an important aspect of counseling it is NOT imperative that the trainee's supervisor:
    a. have specialized training in methods of supervision.
    b. have an in-depth knowledge of the specialty area in which they will provide supervision.
    c. have professional certification in multicultural counseling theory and techniques.
    d. provide timely and adequate supervision while monitoring and evaluating the supervisee's competence.

143. Professional codes of ethics for supervisors agree that:
    a. social interaction with supervisees is essential to effective counselor training.
    b. all dual or multiple relationships with supervisees are unethical.
    c. sexual relationships between supervisors and students are unethical unless the student freely consents.
    d. supervisors occupy a position of power and should not engage in sexual relationships with the student.

144. Below are common characteristics of consultation EXCEPT for which of the following?
    a. The consultant provides indirect service to the client by providing direct serve to consultees to better serve their own clients.
    b. Consultees have the freedom to decide what they will do with the suggestions and recommendations of the consultee.
    c. Participation in the consultation process is often involuntary if the contract is initiated by a program director.
    d. Consultants can take on a variety of roles depending on the nature of consultation and the desired outcomes of consultation.
    e. Consultation typically occurs in an organizational context.

145. The existing ethics codes of the various professional organizations:
    a. do not sufficiently address the complexity of ethical issues consultants encounter.
    b. provide clear directions for consultants.
    c. address multicultural issues in consultation.
    d. specifically state that consultants are expected to establish a written contract with consultees prior to beginning consultation.

CHAPTER 10 ISSUES IN THEORY, PRACTICE, AND RESEARCH

146. Contemporary theories of counseling:
    a. are based on worldviews, each with its own values.
    b. are grounded in assumptions that are part of Western culture.
    c. emphasize choice, uniqueness of the individual, self-assertion, and ego strength.
    d. all of the above
    e. none of the above

147. A(n) _____ is based on a negotiation between the client and the therapists to define the therapeutic relationship.
    a. agreement
    b. contract
    c. covenant
    d. legally enforceable arrangement

148. Which of the following is NOT accurate pertaining to therapeutic goals in a managed care system?
   a. Goals need to be highly specific.
   b. Goals are defined by the managed care program for the client.
   c. Goals are limited to reduction of problematic symptoms.
   d. Goals are likely to be short term and practical.
   e. Goals are aimed at teaching clients coping skills.

149. Which of the following statements in NOT accurate pertaining to the use of techniques?
   a. Practitioners should have a rationale for using a technique.
   b. Practitioners need to have training in the proper use of techniques.
   c. There is abundant evidence of the specific value and usefulness of particular techniques.
   d. The techniques counselors employ are less crucial to therapy outcomes than are the interpersonal factors operating in the client-counselor relationship.

150. The main purpose of the diagnostic approach is to:
   a. make clients feel better.
   b. allow the therapist to plan treatments tailored to the special needs of the client.
   c. identify a category for insurance payments to clients.
   d. protect the therapist from malpractice.
   e. provide an aura of professionalism for the therapist.

151. Which is an argument *for* diagnosis?
   a. Diagnosis facilitates the selection of the most suitable form of therapy.
   b. Diagnosis can increase the chance of a malpractice suit.
   c. Diagnosis can rob people of their uniqueness.
   d. Diagnosis can lead people to accept self-fulfilling prophecies.

152. Which is an argument *against* diagnosis?
   a. Diagnostic classifications facilitate administrative tasks.
   b. Diagnosis enables therapists to make appropriate treatment plans.
   c. Diagnosis can narrow the therapist's vision by encouraging the therapist to look for behavior that fits a certain disease category.
   d. Diagnosis is required by managed care systems.
   e. Diagnosis provides a framework for research.

153. The _____ is based on the assumption that greater attention needs to be paid to environmental and contextual issues as it applies to assessment and diagnosis.
   a. psychoanalytic approach
   b. humanistic approach
   c. behavioristic model
   d. developmental counseling and therapy model

154. _____ is the process of distinguishing one form of disease or psychological disorder from another by determining which of two (or more) diseases or disorders with similar symptoms the person is suffering from.
   a. Medical diagnosis
   b. Differential diagnosis
   c. Clinical diagnosis
   d. Psychological diagnosis

155. _____ is the process of evaluating the relevant factors in a client's life to identify themes for further exploration in the counseling process.
   a. Writing a contract
   b. An assessment
   c. Psychological orientation
   d. Psychodiagnosis

156. The position of the authors on assessment and psychodiagnosis is best captured by which statement(s)?
    a. Assessment and diagnosis can help practitioners conceptualize a case and implement treatment.
    b. Diagnosis is a process of thinking about the client with the client.
    c. Diagnosis can be viewed as a general descriptive statement identifying a client's behavioral style.
    d. all of the above
    e. none of the above

157. The managed care model stresses:
    a. remediation of deeply-rooted personal problems.
    b. long-term interventions.
    c. curative strategies rather than preventive strategies.
    d. cost-effective methods.

158. Which of the following is NOT considered to be a critical ethical issue associated with managed care?
    a. informed consent
    b. the therapeutic relationship
    c. confidentiality
    d. utilization review
    e. abandonment

159. Perhaps the most basic ethical guideline for using tests is to:
    a. use tests that will tell clients what they should do.
    b. encourage clients to believe in any tests they take.
    c. provide objective measures that will help clients make better decisions.
    d. select the one best test for the client.

160. Informed consent for research participants entails the element of:
    a. competence.
    b. full information.
    c. comprehension.
    d. all of the above

CHAPTER 11 ETHICAL ISSUES IN COUPLES AND FAMILY THERAPY

161. Gender-aware therapy is primarily aimed at:
    a. helping men and women to adjust to social norms of appropriate sex-role behavior.
    b. helping clients understand how societal conceptions of gender often limit their thinking, feeling, and behaving.
    c. developing techniques to get women clients to become more assertive.
    d. encouraging clients to become politically involved in changing gender-based discrimination.

162. If counselors are working with families, and if their program did not prepare them for competence in family therapy, they are:
    a. vulnerable to a malpractice suit.
    b. doing what they must do under the circumstances.
    c. on safe ground as long as the family knows about their limited training.
    d. doing the appropriate thing if an individual client requests family therapy sessions.

163. An example of experiential methods of training in family therapy is:
    a. listening to class lectures on family systems.
    b. observing family therapy sessions and taking notes.
    c. working with one's own family of origin.
    d. doing readings in family therapy.
    e. none of the above are experiential.

164. The AAMFT *Code of Ethics* contains statements about each of the following areas except for:
    a. confidentiality.
    b. requiring personal therapy for family therapy trainees.
    c. professional competence and integrity.
    d. fees.
    e. responsibility to students, employees, and supervisees.

165. Regarding the matter of fees for professional services, the AAMFT codes specify that family therapists:
a. do not accept payment for making referrals.
b. do not become involved with third party payors.
c. never change their fee structure during the time they work with a given family.
d. must have clients sign a document that states that they understand the policies pertaining to payment for services.
e. none of the above

166. Regarding confidentiality in the practice of family therapy, the authors contend that therapists should explain to the family:
a. that there is no confidentiality within the structure of the family therapy sessions.
b. that all secrets must be disclosed.
c. that confidentiality of individuals is respected, if the information is obtained in a session with the individual alone.
d. that confidentiality does not apply in cases involving extramarital affairs.
e. their position on confidentiality from the outset of therapy.

167. The function of the family therapist is to:
a. make decisions regarding how members of the family need to change.
b. help family members evaluate how well their patterns are working and encourage them to make necessary changes.
c. take sides with one member of the family against another.
d. impose their values on family members.

168. Women who seek therapy are NOT likely to need assistance with:
a. overcoming dependency.
b. learning to make autonomous choices.
c. learning to share their feelings with others.
d. raising their self-esteem.

169. A therapy perspective that encourages personal commitment to change gender inequity, and espouses a vision of a future society that values equality between women and men is:
a. feminist therapy.
b. "gender-aware" therapy.
c. non-sexist therapy.
d. androgynous therapy.

170. When family therapists take the time to obtain informed consent from everyone in the family, they convey the message that:
a. no family member should leave until therapy is terminated.
b. no one member is seen as the source of all the family's problems, the "identified patient".
c. the family is aware of the fee structure and able to pay for their therapy.
d. there are limits to confidentiality that will probably hinder therapy.

CHAPTER 12 ETHICAL ISSUES IN GROUP WORK

171. The ASGW *Professional Standards for Training Group Workers* calls for:
a. required individual therapy for trainees.
b. required group therapy for trainees.
c. a minimum number of hours of supervised practice in leading groups.
d. achieving a passing score on an objective test on group counseling.
e. a doctorate in counseling psychology.

172. Concerning the matter of the psychological risks involved in participating in a group, ethical practice demands that leaders:
a. make sure that their groups are risk free.
b. insist on members signing a contract stating they are willing to incur any potential risks or negative outcomes of a group.
c. take precautionary measures to reduce unnecessary psychological risks.
d. consult with an attorney to determine if these risks might make leaders vulnerable to malpractice suits.

173. Which of the following is NOT considered an ethical issue related to an ongoing therapeutic group?
    a. the impact of the therapist's values on the group
    b. protecting members from unnecessary risks
    c. being alert for symptoms of psychological debilitation in group members
    d. maintaining confidentiality
    e. making sure the group is homogeneous in population

174. Group leaders who fail to screen potential members for their groups are:
    a. highly unethical in all circumstances.
    b. guilty of illegal practices.
    c. behaving in highly unprofessional ways, and are likely to be sued.
    d. more likely to include a group member who may not function well in the group setting.

175. Confidentiality in groups:
    a. is not protected by law in most states.
    b. can be legally assured if the group leader is a licensed professional.
    c. presents no ethical dilemmas.
    d. can be guaranteed for the members at the first session.

176. Involuntary group participation:
    a. is clearly unethical.
    b. is always an invasion of the rights of clients.
    c. is illegal in most states.
    d. can be ethical if informed consent procedures are followed.

177. There are many advantages to the co-leader model for groups. All below are true EXCEPT for which statement:
    a. Co-leaders can complement and balance each other.
    b. Co-leaders can share the responsibilities of group.
    c. It is essential that co-leaders always share the same perceptions or interpretations.
    d. The choice of a co-leader is crucial to effective group functioning.

178. The following is *true* concerning the group experience:
    a. The group leader can guarantee that all members will respect the confidentiality rule.
    b. Members may experience disruptions in their lives as a result of their work in group.
    c. The legal concept of privileged communication generally applies in a group setting.
    d. Group members need to be coerced into participating in exercises that will benefit them.

179. The primary reason that therapy groups fit well into the managed care scene is because they:
    a. can be designed to be brief and cost-effective treatments.
    b. provide a sense of community to serve as an antidote to an impersonal culture in which many clients live.
    c. serve the purpose of teaching interpersonal skills.
    d. provide a natural laboratory that demonstrates to people that they are not alone and there is hope for creating a different life.

180. The current trend in training for group workers focuses on learning group process by:
    a. didactic course work.
    b. becoming involved in supervised experiences.
    c. administering psychological tests to trainees.
    d. all of the above

181. The *Professional Training Standards of Group Workers* specify:
    a. a set of core knowledge.
    b. skill competencies.
    c. both knowledge and skill competencies.
    d. specialized training for advanced group leadership.

182. As a way to train effective group workers, the authors recommend all of the following EXCEPT for:
   a. personal (private) psychotherapy.
   b. experience in group therapy, group counseling, or a personal-growth group.
   c. recognition that professional codes, legislative mandates, and institutional policies alone will ensure competent group leadership.
   d. participation in a supervision and training group.

183. Which of the following is NOT considered to be one of the characteristics of diversity sensitive group work?
   a. Group counselors respect members' religious and spiritual beliefs and values.
   b. Group counselors respect the roles of family and community hierarchies within a client's culture.
   c. Group counselors treat all members the same.
   d. Group counselors acquire the knowledge and skills necessary for working with diverse clients.

184. The following is true in regards to group ethics:
   a. As a rule, group leaders should conduct only those types of groups for which they have been trained.
   b. The legal concept of privileged communication applies in group settings the same as it applies to individual sessions.
   c. Group leaders are not obliged to inform psychiatric hospital patients that they are documenting group sessions.
   d. Parents and guardians have the legal right to all communications that have occurred in groups for minors.

185. Below is an example of a technique being used in an unethical way:
   a. modifying techniques so they are suitable for the client's cultural and ethnic background.
   b. practicing unfamiliar techniques in group.
   c. have a therapeutic purpose and be grounded in some theoretical framework.
   d. members are given the freedom on whether or not they wish participate in a given experiment.

CHAPTER 13 ETHICAL ISSUES IN COMMUNITY WORK

186. The community mental-health worker focuses primarily on:
   a. the early crises in an individual's life and how they were resolved.
   b. the person-in-the-environment.
   c. the quality of the bonding that took place between the child and the mother.
   d. using traditional approaches to bring about changes with at-risk clients.
   e. finding ways to include the family of origin in any individual's therapeutic plan.

187. The community counselor who works to empower disenfranchised groups such as the homeless, the handicapped, and AIDS victims illustrates:
   a. direct community services in the form of preventive education.
   b. indirect community services aimed at changing the social environment by influencing policymakers.
   c. direct client services focusing on outreach activities to an at-risk population.
   d. indirect client services of client advocacy involving active intervention on the behalf of an individual or a group.

188. Programs such as life-planning workshops, value-clarification seminars, and interpersonal-skills training are examples of:
   a. direct community services in the form of preventive education.
   b. indirect community services aimed at changing the social environment by influencing policymakers.
   c. direct client services focusing on outreach activities to an at-risk population.
   d. indirect client services consisting of client advocacy involving active intervention on the behalf of an individual or a group.

189. When counselors go into the community and develop programs to help clients deal with stressors that impair their coping ability, such as employee assistance and substance-abuse treatment, this illustrates:
a. direct community services in the form of preventive education.
b. indirect community services aimed at changing the social environment by influencing policymakers.
c. direct client services focusing on outreach activities to an at-risk population.
d. indirect client services consisting of client advocacy involving active intervention on the behalf of an individual or a group.

190. Counselors who attempt to change the social environment by transforming social policy illustrate:
a. direct community services in the form of preventive education.
b. indirect community services aimed at changing the social environment by influencing policymakers.
c. direct client services focusing on outreach activities to an at-risk population.
d. indirect client services consisting of client advocacy involving active intervention on the behalf of an individual or a group.

191. The trend toward the increased use of nonlicensed practitioners means that:
a. mental-health professionals can be expected to spend more time in providing direct services to clients.
b. professionals will have to assume new and expanding roles.
c. all direct services will be performed by nonlicensed workers.
d. the public is likely to get inferior services.

192. The system may be so cumbersome and difficult for clients to work with that counselors often need to assist their clients by adopting the role of:
a. consultant.
b. advocate.
c. adviser.
d. facilitator of indigenous support systems.
e. all of the above

193. According to the authors, those practitioners who work within a system:
a. are almost certain to experience burnout.
b. are challenged to learn how to make the system work both for themselves and their clients.
c. cannot remain in the system and also retain their integrity and dignity.
d. must learn to take advantage of the system through manipulation of those in power.

194. _____ are attempts to change the social environment to meet the needs of he population as a whole and are carried out by influencing social policy.
a. Direct community services
b. Indirect community services
c. Community organization services
d. Community counseling services

195. Direct client services focuses on:
a. outreach activities.
b. client advocacy.
c. consultation.
d. influencing policymakers.

196. Counselors who work in the community need to recognize that it would be an error to:
a. use community resources as a way to enrich therapy.
b. believe that one person or group has a monopoly on the helping process.
c. work with client problems in their cultural context.
d. attend to the network of the client's support systems.

197. In which role do counselors assist clients in recognizing oppressive forces in the community as a source of their problem and teach their clients strategies for developing political power to bring about change in the clients' social and physical environment?
a. change agent
b. consultant
c. adviser
d. advocate

198. Counselors can encourage ethnic minority clients to learn skills they can use to interact successfully with various forces in their community by acting as their:
   a. advocate.
   b. broker.
   c. adviser.
   d. consultant.

199. Lay volunteers from the community receive thirty hours of training before working in the abuse shelter. They receive supervision at the site and are considered to be:
   a. indigenous workers.
   b. nonlicensed workers.
   c. counseling professionals.
   d. professional community service worker.

200. In a community setting, case management is:
   a. guided by the principles of collaboration.
   b. based on a holistic perspective.
   c. geared to providing effective and efficient delivery of services.
   d. all of the above
   e. none of the above

Answer Key for
FINAL EXAM for Issues and Ethics in the Helping Professions, Sixth Edition

CHAPTER 1

1. c
2. b
3. d
4. c
5. c
6. a
7. a
8. a
9. c
10. c
11. a
12. d
13. b
14. d
15. b

CHAPTER 2
16. a
17. d
18. b
19. d
20. c
21. b
22. d
23. b
24. b
25. b
26. a
27. b
28. c
29. a
30. e

CHAPTER 3
31. c
32. b
33. d
34. b
35. c
36. c
37. c
38. e
39. b
40. b

CHAPTER 4
41. c
42. a
43. b
44. d
45. c
46. a
47. c
48. d
49. b
50. b
51. e
52. c

53. b
54. a
55. c

CHAPTER 5
56. d
57. c
58. a
59. b
60. c
61. a
62. b
63. d
64. e
65. b
66. e
67. a
68. a
69. c
70. b
71. c
72. c
73. e
74. e
75. a
76. d
77. d
78. a
79. d
80. c

CHAPTER 6
81. b
82. a
83. c
84. b
85. d
86. b
87. b
88. b
89. d
90. e
91. b
92. b
93. a
94. d
95. c
96. e
97. a
98. c
99. c
100. b

CHAPTER 7
101. a
102. b
103. d
104. e
105. c
106. a

107. e
108. e
109. c
110. b
111. d
112. c
113. a
114. d
115. c

CHAPTER 8
116. b
117. e
118. a
119. a
120. d
121. c
122. c
123. c
124. d
125. a
126. a
127. d
128. b
129. c
130. a

PART 7

ONLINE QUIZ ITEMS for
Issues and Ethics in the Helping
Professions, Sixth Edition

CHAPTER 1 INTRODUCTION TO PROFESSIONAL ETHICS

C-9   1. An example of having potential conflict between legal and ethical standards pertains to breaking confidentiality of a client who:

    a.   is HIV-positive by informing third parties that they are at risk for contacting the virus.
    b.   confides that they have abused their child.
    c.   is a threat to self or others.
    d.   has given written consent.

F-12   2. _____ describes a level of ethical functioning in which the counselor merely acts in compliance with minimal standards.

    a.   Basic ethics
    b.   Mandatory ethics
    c.   Aspirational ethics
    d.   Principles ethics

A-17   3. James is using his client's test scores to assess the effectiveness of various methods of counseling. He plans to write a book on his work but does not inform his clients that their test results will be used as a basis of his book. James is violating the following moral principle of ethical decision making:

    a.   fidelity
    b.   justice
    c.   veracity
    d.   autonomy

F-20   4. The first essential step towards ethical decision making is:

    a.   defining the problem.
    b.   choosing a solution.
    c.   identifying the problem or dilemma.
    d.   developing a solution.
    e.   reviewing the process.

C-20   5. The following step of ethical decision making is critical in matters of keeping or breaching confidentiality, reporting child or elder abuse, record keeping, test and assessment, diagnosis, and grounds for malpractice:

    a.   Know the applicable laws and regulations.
    b.   Obtain written consent.
    c.   Enumerate the consequences of various decisions.
    d.   Consider possible and probable courses of action.

True-False
In taking the true-false questions for each of these chapters, decide if the statement is "more true" or "more false." The (number) indicates the page in the text in which the item is found. T=True and F=False.

(6)   6. The ethics codes of most of the professional organizations are precise and specific, rather than broad and general.

(7)   7. Ethics codes tend to be proactive rather than reactive.

(8)   8. Ethical issues in the mental health professions are regulated by both laws and professional codes.

(13)   9. Virtue ethics focuses on the character traits of the counselor and nonobligatory ideals to which professionals aspire.

(18)   10. Ethical decision making is primarily a cognitive and linear and step by step process.

CHAPTER 2 THE COUNSELOR AS A PERSON AND AS A PROFESSIONAL

F-45   1. The negative consequences that conducting therapy can have on practitioners' interpersonal functioning include all of the following EXCEPT for which of the following?

a. decreased emotional investment in their families
b. a tendency to socialize a great deal with friends
c. a reduction in the circle of friends
d. a tendency to become aloof and emotionally distant with family and friends

C-53   2. Some clinicians believe they should be available to take all messages from their clients, and they have every voice mail or answering machine messages paged to them. Clinicians who engage in this behavior are likely:

a. increase the chances of a malpractice suit.
b. decrease the chances of a malpractice suit.
c. promote client dependence.
d. promote the client's autonomy.

A-51   3. Joe sees his female client as needy and dependent just like he remembers his mother's behavior when he was growing up. Joe dislikes these characteristics and countertransference is likely to manifest itself in the following manner:

a. treating his client in benign ways
b. being overprotective with his client
c. rejecting his client
d. giving advice

C-53   4. Counselors who encourages dependence on the part of their clients may do so because they have a need:

a. to feel important.
b. for approval.
c. for constant reinforcement and approval.
d. to compulsively give advice.
e. develop social relationships with their clients.

C-62   5. Ethical codes on professional impairment suggest the following guidance for practitioners:

a. Take a reactive stance that focuses on the result of emotional distress rather than a proactive stance.
b. Seek immediate consultation to determine whether they should limit, suspend, or terminate the relationship.
c. Avoid confrontation from colleagues while engaging in an ongoing process of self-assessment.
d. Seek social relationships with clients to alleviate professional isolation.

True-False
In taking the true-false questions for each of these chapters, decide if the statement is "more true" or "more false." The (number) indicates the page in the text in which the item is found. T=True and F=False.

(45)   6. It is illegal for state licensing boards to require therapy as a way for therapists to recognize and monitor their countertransference.

(46)   7. If a client experiences transference toward a therapist, this is a good indication that this client should be referred to another therapist.

(48)   8. Countertransference can be considered either a constructive or destructive element in the therapeutic relationship.

(60)   9. A growing body of research suggests that many therapists experience negative effects with respect to their ability to relate meaningfully with family and friends.

(67)   10. Self-care is not a luxury, but an ethical mandate.

CHAPTER 3 VALUES AND THE HELPING RELATIONSHIP

C-85   1. All of these statements concerning the role of spiritual and religious values in counseling are true EXCEPT one of the following?

    a.   There is now widespread interest in how spiritual and religious beliefs might be incorporated in therapeutic relationships.
    b.   The major professional organizations are increasingly recognizing the importance of spiritual issues in counseling practice.
    c.   For many clients, spirituality and religion are critical sources of strength and can be instrumental in promoting healing and well-being.
    d.   One survey reveals that 96% of psychologists believe that religious faith is important in their own lives.

A-81   2. Joe is an elderly man who has just been moved to a nursing home and is experiencing feelings of loss, sadness and hopelessness. He is assigned a young social worker who recently graduated from college. She will need to provide some services to help him adjust to his new environment. Joe seems to be reluctant to speak to her. In this case, Joe needs to:

    a.   be referred to a more experienced professional.
    b.   speak to a nurse about his problems.
    c.   understand that she can empathize with him because she has had similar feelings even though her experiences were different.
    d.   demand that he get the services he needs without talking to his social worker.

C-85   3. When working with clients, it is important to remember that spirituality or religion:

    a.   may enter into the sessions indirectly as the client explores moral conflicts or grapples with the meaning of life.
    b.   should never be brought into the counseling process.
    c.   is comparable to counseling in all respects.
    d.   should be seen as a defense mechanism

C-91   4. Counselors need to be aware that when they introduce religious themes, there is a potential for:

    a.   converting their client.
    b.   avoiding secularism.
    c.   countertransference.
    d.   transference.

F-97   5. According to the National Association of Social Workers (NASW, 1994), individuals have a choice regarding continuing care or treatment options when they have a terminal illness. This does NOT include:

    a.   immediate hospitalization for suicide ideation.
    b.   physician-assisted suicide.
    c.   aggressive treatment of the medical condition.
    d.   withholding or withdrawing life-sustaining treatment.
    e.   voluntary active euthanasia.

True-False
In taking the true-false questions for each of these chapters, decide if the statement is "more true" or "more false." The (number) indicates the page in the text in which the item is found. T=True and F=False.

(76)   6. It is now generally accepted that the therapeutic endeavor is a value-laden process and that all therapists, to some degree, communicate their values to clients.

(76)   7. Merely having a conflict of values does not necessarily require a referral; it is possible to work through such conflicts successfully.

(81)   8. To work effectively with clients, it is generally essential for counselors to have experienced the same problem as the clients to seek help.

(85)   9. There is a growing awareness and willingness to explore spiritual and religious matters within the context of counselor education programs.

(93)   10. Most mental health practitioners do not believe that it is essential to include a client's religious believes in the assessment and treatment practice.

CHAPTER 4 MULTICULTURAL PERSPECTIVES AND DIVERSITY ISSUES

C-112   1. Counselors practice unintentional racism when they:

a. show sensitivity to cultural variations among individuals.
b. challenge stereotypes associated with culturally diverse clients.
c. claim to be free of any traces of racism.
d. accept unreasoned assumptions about other cultures without proof and without regard to rationality.

F-111   2. _____ goes beyond the concerns of the individual to address the consequences   of racism, and poverty, and discrimination on minority groups and aims to change institutions that perpetuate these conditions.

a. Client-centered therapy
b. Diversity-sensitive counseling
c. Minority group counseling
d. Community counseling

F-126   3. Which of the following statements is FALSE?

a. It is important to understand that homosexuality and bisexuality are not indicative of mental illness.
b. The ethics codes of the ACA, the APA, and the NASW clearly state that discrimination on the basis of sexual orientation is unethical and unacceptable.
c. Therapists have an ethical obligation to confront their personal prejudices, myths, fears, and stereotypes regarding sexual orientation.
d. To date the APA has not developed a separate set of guidelines for psychotherapy with lesbian, gay, and bisexual clients.

A-124   4. Mary is working with an Asian client. She uses a confrontational style that involves direct eye contact, physical gestures, and probing personal questions. Her style is likely to be perceived by the client as:

a. offensively intrusive.
b. directive and helpful.
c. unethical.
d. the counselor's attempt to create a positive therapeutic relationship.

C-138   5. Below is an ineffective strategy for counselors working with multicultural clients:

a. Be willing to contrast their own beliefs and attitudes with those of their clients in a nonjudgmental fashion.
b. Understand the sociopolitical influences that impinge on the lives of racial and ethnic minorities.
c. Have knowledge of potential bias in assessment instruments and interpret accordingly.
d. Develop a non-racist identity by socializing with culturally diverse clients.

True-False
In taking the true-false questions for each of these chapters, decide if the statement is "more true" or "more false." The (number) indicates the page in the text in which the item is found. T=True and F=False.

(115)   6. At the present time, most ethics codes fail to make specific mention of a practitioner's responsibility to recognize the special needs of diverse client populations.

(116)   7. Ethical guidelines appropriate in one cultural context may not be appropriate in contrasting cultural settings.

(117)   8. Some writers believe that the diversity-sensitive counseling movement lacks moderation and attempts to superimpose its agenda on counseling practice.

(124)   9. If a client avoids making direct eye contact with the counselor, it is likely that this client is being evasive or resistant.

(125)   10. The American Psychiatric Association still considers homosexuality as a form of mental illness.

92

CHAPTER 5 CLIENT RIGHTS AND COUNSELOR RESPONSIBILITIES

C-149   1. An informed consent document should NOT attempt to:

    a.   define the risks associated with counseling.
    b.   specify how confidentiality will be handled in counseling.
    c.   guarantee results of counseling.
    d.   indicate that there may be frequent consultation with other mental health professional regarding the management of the client's case.

C-158   2. Jason is going to a counselor in a managed care setting. His therapeutic process will probably be determined by the:

    a.   counselor.
    b.   client.
    c.   both the counselor and the client.
    d.   health provider.

C-159   3. One of the major obstacles of allowing clients to read their files is that:

    a.   third parties often require diagnostic classifications before reimbursement and may be misinterpreted by the client.
    b.   records often contain misleading information that could confuse the client.
    c.   clients' charts are likely to contain judgmental statements that could lead to a lawsuit.
    d.   clients are unlikely to understand the professional jargon used by counselors.

C170   4. Which of the following is NOT considered a benefit of delivering counseling services online?

    a.   providing brief, convenient, and anonymous therapy service
    b.   assuring confidentiality and privacy
    c.   increasing flexibility in scheduling
    d.   increasing options for supervision and case conferencing

C-174   5. The parent's right to information about his or her child:

    a.   is mandatory by law.
    b.   should not be disclosed to the child because it will hinder the counseling relationship.
    c.   entitles the parent to general information from the counselor about the child's progress in counseling.
    d.   gives parents the right to access all of their child's records.

True-False
In taking the true-false questions for each of these chapters, decide if the statement is "more true" or "more false." The (number) indicates the page in the text in which the item is found. T=True and F=False.

(155)   6. Practitioners can be assured that they can avoid legal action if they obtain written informed consent from their clients.

(158)   7. Clients have a right to know how their health care program is likely to influence the course of their therapy as well as the limitations imposed by the program.

(165)   8. If a mental health practitioner acts reasonably and keeps good records, he or she cannot be sued.

(166)   9. The client's clinical record belongs to the client, and a copy of this record may be requested at any time.

(171)   10. Recently, most state legislatures have addressed ethical and legal parameters of Internet counseling.

CHAPTER 6 CONFIDENTIALITY: ETHICAL AND LEGAL ISSUES

C-205 1. Exceptions to the legal concept of confidentiality and therapist-client privilege include all but one of the following:

    a.   The client consents to disclosure.
    b.   There is a duty to warn or protect third parties.
    c.   Reimbursement or other legal rules require disclosure.
    d.   The therapist wants to use the case as an example for trainees without the informed consent of the client.
    e.   An emergency exists.

C-209 2. Practitioners are generally NOT legally liable for:

    a.   failure to render perfect predictions of violent behavior of a client.
    b.   failing to commit dangerous individuals.
    c.   prematurely discharging dangerous clients from a hospital.
    d.   failing to warn potential victims of violent behavior.

A-212 3. Joe's wife expressed fear that her abusive husband would eventually kill her. Joe agreed to a psychiatric evaluation and it was determined that he wasn't dangerous. Joe beat his wife again and was brought back to the therapist for another evaluation. Joe was released after a brief interview and he promptly went home and killed her. Joe's therapist is liable for a malpractice suit according to the following court ruling:

    a.   Tarasoff case
    b.   Bradley case
    c.   Jablonski case
    d.   Hedlund case
    e.   Jaffee case

C-217 4. In an attempt to limit the therapist liability, documentation should:

    a.   not be written because the records may be subpoenaed into court if the client actually harms another individual.
    b.   be used as a risk management strategy and include a brief statement of the rationale for the actions taken to protect.
    c.   be altered if they are subpoenaed into court and could result in a malpractice suit.
    d.   be manufactured after the fact if the counselor has kept poor records.

C-228 5. Maria had a child as a result of a rape and has admitted that she has abused her son because he is a reminder of the painful experience that led to his birth. Maria is in therapy trying to deal with the rage she feels towards the rapist and hopes that this will help towards developing a healthier relationship with her son. In this case, the counselor needs to:

    a.   help the mother overcome her rage and warn her that the abuse will be reported if it continues.
    b.   report the abuse.
    c.   suggest that the mother put her child in foster care until she has dealt with her rage.
    d.   work on her issues with her child after dealing with the rape.

True-False
In taking the true-false questions for each of these chapters, decide if the statement is "more true" or "more false." The (number) indicates the page in the text in which the item is found. T=True and F=False.

(196) 6. Confidentiality is a legal concept and privileged communication is an ethical concept.

(198) 7. Generally, privileged communication applies to group counseling, couples counseling, and family therapy if the practitioner is a licensed psychologist.

(199) 8. A clear judicial trend has emerged for communications that are made in the presence of third persons.

(203) 9. Parents and guardians have some legal right to request information about counseling sessions, but minors have an ethical right to expect confidentiality in the relationship.

(209) 10. Currently, only a few states permit therapists to breach confidentiality to warn or protect victims.

CHAPTER 7 MANAGING BOUNDARIES AND MULTIPLE RELATIONSHIPS

F-249   1. The theoretical perspective that maintains   that transference, countertransference, resistance, and interpretation necessarily involve some form of dual relationship in counseling is:

    a.   rational emotive behavior therapy.
    b.   client-centered therapy.
    c.   reality therapy.
    d.   psychoanalytic therapy.

C-265   2. A reason for discouraging the practice of accepting friends as clients or becoming socially involved with clients is that counselors:

    a.   are more likely to confront clients they know socially.
    b.   may have a need to be liked which could lead them to be less challenging lest the relationship be jeopardized.
    c.   tend to be too objective with clients that they know personally.
    d.   need a social life away from work.

C-270   3. Below would be an inappropriate response from a therapist who is struggling with a powerful attraction to a client:

    a.   Seek out an experienced colleague, supervisor, or therapist who might help decide a course of action.
    b.   Monitor boundaries by setting clear limits on physical contact and self-disclosure.
    c.   Repress feelings of attraction to protect oneself from becoming sexually involved with the client.
    d.   Explore reasons for attraction to the client.

F-273   4. The statement below is NOT true in regards to sexual contact between therapist and client:

    a.   Sexual misconduct is the most common allegation in malpractice suits.
    b.   The majority of sexual boundary violations occurs between female therapists and male clients.
    c.   Sexual misconduct is considered to be one of the most serious of all ethical violations for a therapist.
    d.   Sexual conduct with clients is prohibited in codes of ethics of various professional organizations.
    e.   Many ethical codes specify that if the therapist had prior sexual contact with a person, they should not accept them as clients.

A-283   5. Robert's client is a mother who is deeply grieving over the death of her child. Robert feels compassionate as he gently touches her arm to show her that he cares. His client seems comforted by the action, yet he has failed to ask permission to touch. In this case, Robert:

    a.   is likely to have his action misinterpreted as sexually exploitative.
    b.   is unprofessional and has invaded the client's boundaries.
    c.   is likely to create dependency in the counseling relationship.
    d.   expressed empathy for the client that would not be considered unethical by most practitioners.

True-False
In taking the true-false questions for each of these chapters, decide if the statement is "more true" or "more false." The (number) indicates the page in the text in which the item is found. T=True and F=False.

(251)   6. Role blending is clearly unethical, since it generally involves a conflict of interest.

(252)   7. The trend in state licensure boards has been to prohibit all dual relationships, including nonsexual dual relationships.

(258)   8. Because the practice of bartering is fought with potential problems and possible harm to clients, this practice is considered unethical by most professional organizations.

(262)   9. Within the last 10 years, most of the codes of ethics of various professional organizations specifically address the topic of giving or receiving gifts in the therapeutic relationship.

(279)   10. Many clients do not know that sexual contact between counselors and client is unethical and illegal.

CHAPTER 8 PROFESSIONAL COMPETENCE AND TRAINING

C-302   1. Programs geared to educating and training counselors need to start with a:

    a.   well designed curriculum that includes multicultural training.
    b.   supervised fieldwork experiences.
    c.   systematic coverage of ethical issues.
    d.   foundation of natural talents and abilities of the student.

C-306   2. Counseling programs can be held legally liable for counselors who graduated from their program and:

    a.   prove to be incompetent.
    b.   are involved in dual relationships with their clients.
    c.   received good grades, yet were in therapy to deal with some personal problems.
    d.   practiced as a specialist in an area that they were not trained in.

F-308   3. _____ is generally viewed as the most desirable form of legislative regulation of professional practice because it restricts both the use of the title and the practice of an occupation.

    a.   Licensure
    b.   Certification
    c.   Registration
    d.   Accreditation

A-296   4. Jim is seeing a women who is in counseling over issues concerning her teenaged son. After counseling her on an individual basis, he asks to see both of them together. Jim suspects that his client's son may be chemically dependent, although he is not trained in this area. In this case, Jim needs to:

    a.   work with the mother to help her deal with her son's chemical abuse issues.
    b.   refer the son to a chemical dependency counselor for an assessment.
    c.   refer the son to an in-patient treatment center.
    d.   continue to see both of them together to work on enhancing their relationship.

C-310   5. An argument used against legislation to regulate the delivery of mental-health services is that:

    a.   the public is protected by setting minimum standards of service and holding professionals accountable.
    b.   insurance companies frequently reimburse clients for the service of licensed practitioners allowing more people to receive mental-health care.
    c.   certification contributes to professional specializations that pit one against the other.
    d.   licensure is perceived to enhance the profession by defining for itself what it will and will not do.

True-False
In taking the true-false questions for each of these chapters, decide if the statement is "more true" or "more false." The (number) indicates the page in the text in which the item is found. T=True and F=False.

(304)   6. Evaluating trainees' knowledge and skills should be limited to their knowledge and skills.

(306)   7. Professional training programs can be held legally liable for turning out incompetent practitioners.

(308)   8. Licensure acts specify what the holder of the license can do and what others cannot do.

(311)   9. Most mental health professionals still do not have to complete a minimal number of continuing education activities as a condition for relicensure or recertification.

(304)   10. Assessing graduate students to determine whether they have the knowledge and skills required to function effectively as practitioners is essential.

CHAPTER 9 ISSUES IN SUPERVISION AND CONSULTATION

C-323   1. The authors believe that the most important element in the supervisory process is the supervisor's ability to:

a.   teach methods and techniques that are up-to-date.
b.   establish an effective collaborative working relationship with supervisees.
c.   use a directive style of supervision.
d.   be an effective therapist for their trainees.

F-328   2. Supervisors in counseling training programs bear both direct liability and vicarious liability. Vicarious liability pertains to:

a.   derelict supervision of trainees.
b.   inappropriate advice given to trainees about treatment.
c.   responsibilities that supervisors have because of the actions of their trainees.
d.   giving tasks to trainees that exceed their competence.

C-338   3. In a national survey on sexual intimacy in counselor education and supervision, it was found that counseling professionals who were sexually involved with a supervisor or an educator during their training later viewed these experiences as:

a.   being more coercive and more harmful to a working relationship than they did at the time.
b.   an experience that they fondly remember.
c.   devastating to the point that they were unable to function effectively as counselors.
d.   something they freely consented to.

C-325   4. The ethical practice of clinical supervisors that is least frequently violated pertains to:

a.   confidentiality is supervision.
b.   performance evaluation and monitoring supervisee activities.
c.   supervisors who fail to differentiate supervision from psychotherapy.
d.   supervisors not being receptive to theoretical approaches other than their own.

A-341   5. Gary is a practicing therapist as well as a part-time supervisor in a counseling program. He is supervising a female student who has excellent skills, yet she has some abuse issues that were triggered when she was working with a victim. Gary decides to use their supervision sessions to focus on her personal problems. The authors take a position that:

a.   the supervisor needed to act as the student's personal therapist so the student could continue in the program.
b.   the trainees' own issues should never be   stimulated by their clients.
c.   the training program is operating unethically since countertransference occurred.
d.   the emphasis of supervision needs to be on the enhancement of supervisees' work with their clients and students need to be referred to personal therapy if needed.

True-False
In taking the true-false questions for each of these chapters, decide if the statement is "more true" or "more false." The (number) indicates the page in the text in which the item is found. T=True and F=False.

(321)   6. Supervisors are ultimately responsible, both ethically and legally, for the actions of their trainees.

(327)   7. It is recommended that supervisors make use of professional disclosure statements for supervision so that supervisees are informed of the potential benefits, risks, and expectations of entering into the supervisory relationship.

(328)   8. If supervisors are derelict in the supervision of their trainees, they can incur vicarious liability.

(335) 9. A hallmark of feminist supervision is that supervisors advance and model the principle of advocacy and activism.

(336) 10. Supervisors who play multiple roles and engage in multiple relationships with supervisees are being unethical.

CHAPTER 10 ISSUES IN THEORY, PRACTICE, AND RESEARCH

F-360 1. _____ therapies are those most likely to emphasize client-initiated contracts and homework assignments as ways in which clients can fulfill the commitment to change.

    a. Multicultural
    b. Humanistic
    c. Directive
    d. Psychoanalytic

F-363 2. _____ is the process of evaluating the relevant factors in a client's life to identify themes for further exploration in the counseling process.

    a. Writing a contract
    b. An assessment
    c. Orientation
    d. Diagnosis

C-365 3. Diagnosis is intended to do all of the following EXCEPT:

    a. point the way to appropriate treatment strategies for specific disorders.
    b. allow the therapist to rule out possible medical conditions for psychological problems.
    c. help the therapist determine whether clients pose a danger to themselves or others.
    d. inform the client of the cost and method of payment, as well as the length and frequency of sessions.
    e. provide a frame work for research into various treatment approaches.

F-362 4. The following is NOT true in regards to techniques used in counseling and therapy:

    a. The use of techniques in counseling and therapy is closely related to the practitioner's theoretical model.
    b. Successful outcome is largely determined by such client characteristics as motivation and   taking responsibility.
    c. There is little evidence of specific efficacy for particular techniques or counseling theories.
    d. Counselor techniques are more important to successful outcome than the client-counselor relationship.

A-384 5. Students were used in a research study on gender differences in body language. They were aware that the research was on communication, yet were not told that they were being videotaped for fear that they would relate to each other differently. In this case, the researcher's deceptive behavior was:

    a. ethically questionable, since most professional codes explicitly state that such a practice is to be avoided.
    b. was ethical because alternative procedures were not feasible.
    c. violated the student's right to voluntarily choose to participate.
    d. was essential to the outcome of the project.

True-False
In taking the true-false questions for each of these chapters, decide if the statement is "more true" or "more false." The (number) indicates the page in the text in which the item is found. T=True and F=False.

(363) 6. The developmental counseling and therapy model is based on the assumption that greater attention needs to be paid to environmental and contextual issues.

(364) 7. Practitioners with a behavioristic orientation tend to be opposed to diagnosis in psychotherapeutic practice.

(367) 8. From the perspective of the authors, assessment and diagnosis are rarely helpful to the practitioner in conceptualizing a case and implementing treatment.

(378)   9. Clients in a managed care plan have a right to know that there may be other forms of treatment, which may be superior to the one they are receiving, which are being denied to them solely for cost-containment reasons.

(380)   10. Practitioners are ultimately responsible to their clients in an HMO system, even if the decisions are made by the managed care system.

CHAPTER 11 ETHICAL ISSUES IN COUPLES AND FAMILY COUNSELING

F-397   1. The AAMFT *Code of Ethics* addresses each of the following areas EXCEPT for:

  a.   responsibility to students and supervisees.
  b.   financial arrangements.
  c.   use of online therapy with couples.
  d.   advertising.

F-402   2. Family therapy training programs use all of the following methods of training EXCEPT for:

  a.   didactic course work.
  b.   observation of a family therapy session behind a one-way mirror.
  c.   videotaping a family session without the permission of every member of the family.
  d.   the use of master therapist videotapes plus trainee tapes for post-session viewing by the trainees and supervisors.

C-408   3. Women who seek therapy are NOT likely to need assistance with:

  a.   overcoming dependency.
  b.   learning to make autonomous choices.
  c.   learning to share their feelings with others.
  d.   raising their self-esteem.

C-408   4. A therapy perspective that encourages personal commitment to change gender inequity, and espouses a vision of a future society that values equality between women and men is:

  a.   feminist therapy.
  b.   "gender-aware" therapy.
  c.   non-sexist therapy.
  d.   androgynous therapy.

C-415   5. When family therapists take the time to obtain informed consent from every member of the family, they convey the message that:

  a.   no family member should leave until therapy is terminated.
  b.   no one member is seen as the source of all the family's problems, the "identified patient".
  c.   the family is aware of the fee structure and able to pay for their therapy.
  d.   there are limits to confidentiality that will probably hinder therapy.

True-False
In taking the true-false questions for each of these chapters, decide if the statement is "more true" or "more false." The (number) indicates the page in the text in which the item is found. T=True and F=False.

(402)   6. Experiential methods are rarely used in the training of couples and family therapists.

(405)   7. In many cases, the role of family therapists is to decide how members of a family should change if they want to create harmony in the family context.

(409)   8. Feminist therapists take a neutral stance with respect to gender roles and power in relationships.

(415)   9. Because family therapists deal with many members of a family, informed consent is not a critical issue in family therapy as it is in individual therapy.

(416)   10. There is no professional agreement on whether it is necessary to see all the family for family therapy to take place.

CHAPTER 12 ETHICAL ISSUES IN GROUP WORK

C-434 1. Concerning confidentiality and online group therapy, some take the position that:

a. therapy can be ethically conducted over the Internet in most circumstances.
b. there is great difficulty in maintaining the confidential nature of a group.
c. there are really no major problems in protecting clients' privacy.
d. such an approach tends to enhance the interactions within a group.

C-422 2. According to the authors, groups:

a. are generally a second-rate therapeutic approach.
b. create an artificial laboratory setting.
c. are powerful because long-term problems of group members may be played out in the group sessions.
d. have greatly decreased in popularity among professionals because of the ethical concerns in group work.

C-426 3. There are many advantages to the co-leader model for groups. All below are true EXCEPT the following:

a. Co-leaders can complement and balance each other.
b. Co-leaders can share the responsibilities of group.
c. It is essential that co-leaders always share the same perceptions or interpretations.
d. The choice of a co-leader is crucial to effective group functioning.

C-431 4. The following is *true* concerning the group experience:

a. The group leader can guarantee that all members will respect the confidentiality rule.
b. Members may experience major disruptions in their lives as a result of their work in group.
c. The legal concept of privileged   communication generally applies in a group setting.
d. Group members need to be coerced into participating in exercises that will benefit them.

A-438 5. Ann is facilitating a woman's issues group and many of the women in her group have avoided dealing with the aftermath of being victimized in an abusive relationship. She decides to use a guided fantasy to explore the pain and rage connected to their abuse. In order to use this technique effectively, she needs to:

a. pressure all members to take part in the experience.
b. encourage catharsis in those members who are reluctant to express their feelings.
c. apply the technique equally to all members, including those with diverse backgrounds.
d. be aware of the potential impact of the technique and be ready to deal with any emotional release.

True-False
In taking the true-false questions for each of these chapters, decide if the statement is "more true" or "more false." The (number) indicates the page in the text in which the item is found. T=True and F=False.

(422) 6. Research confirms that group treatment is more effective than no treatment, yet group therapy does not appear to be superior to other forms of therapy.

(422) 7. Managed behavioral health care does not accept group therapy as a viable therapeutic option.

(423) 8. To date, there are no professional standards for the training of group workers.

(430) 9. According to the authors, group members have a right to leave a group at any time without an explanation for doing so.

(432) 10. The legal concept of privileged communication generally does not apply in a group setting, unless there has been a statutory exception.

CHAPTER 13 ETHICAL ISSUES IN COMMUNITY WORK

C-451   1. Clients who are low in acculturation and need remediation of a problem that results from oppression and discrimination need counselors who will function in the following role:

    a.   community organizer
    b.   behavior changer
    c.   advocate
    d.   outreach worker

A-459   2. Greg is a former addict who has received a chemical dependency practitioner certificate from a community college and is now working in a treatment center helping other addicts. He is working in the role of a:

    a.   nonlicensed worker.
    b.   traditional counselor.
    c.   professional with training as a specialist.
    d.   recovering addict.

C-465   3. The first step toward responding to unacceptable circumstances in an agency is to:

    a.   leave the situation, either by emotionally withdrawing or by physically leaving.
    b.   decide to adjust to an unacceptable situation.
    c.   identify the situation as unacceptable and attempt to change it.
    d.   recognize the need for action.

C-465   4. In regards to agency policies, counselors:

    a.   typically have much to say in the formulation of agency policies.
    b.   are limited in what they can do by the agency's rules and regulations.
    c.   have to "bend the rules" in order to provide needed services for their clients.
    d.   should conform to institutional policies out of fear of losing their positions.

C-461   5. Case management is guided by the principle(s) of:

    a.   fairness.
    b.   accountability.
    c.   collaboration.
    d.   all of the above

True-False
In taking the true-false questions for each of these chapters, decide if the statement is "more true" or "more false." The (number) indicates the page in the text in which the item is found. T=True and F=False.

(448)   6. Central to the community mental health orientation is the notion of community control of psychological services and an emphasis on prevention and early detection.

(449)   7. Client advocacy, which involves active intervention for and with an individual or a group, is an example of direct client services.

(451)   8. Counselors who work in the community are expected to assume a variety of roles such as advocate, change agent, consultant, and adviser.

(461)   9. The overall goals of case management is to promote, restore, or maintain the independent functioning of consumers in the least-restrictive community environment.

(465)   10. When the interests of the agency supercede the interests of the community, the ethical issues are much the same as when a practitioner's interests supercedes the client's interests.

Answer Key for
ONLINE QUIZ ITEMS for Issues and Ethics in the Helping Professions, Sixth Edition

CHAPTER 1
1. a
2. b
3. c
4. c
5. a
6. F
7. F
8. T
9. T
10. F

CHAPTER 2
1. b
2. c
3. c
4. a
5. b
6. F
7. F
8. T
9. T
10. T

CHAPTER 3
1. d
2. c
3. a
4. c
5. a
6. T
7. T
8. F
9. T
10. F

CHAPTER 4
1. c
2. b

3. d
4. a
5. d
6. F
7. T
8. T
9. F
10. F

CHAPTER 5
1. c
2. d
3. a
4. b
5. c
6. F
7. T
8. F
9. T
10. F

CHAPTER 6
1. d
2. a
3. c
4. b
5. b
6. F
7. F
8. F
9. T
10. F

CHAPTER 7
1. d
2. b
3. c
4. b
5. d
6. F

7. T
8. F
9. F
10. T

CHAPTER 8
1. d
2. a
3. b
4. b
5. c
6. F
7. T
8. T
9. F
10. T

CHAPTER 9
1. b
2. c
3. a
4. c
5. d
6. T
7. T
8. F
9. T
10. F

CHAPTER 10
1. c
2. b
3. d
4. d
5. a
6. T
7. F
8. F
9. T
10. T

CHAPTER 11
1. c
2. c
3. c
4. a
5. b
6. F
7. F
8. F
9. F
10. T

CHAPTER 12
1. b
2. c
3. c
4. b
5. d
6. T
7. F
8. F
9. F
10. T

CHAPTER 13
1. c
2. a
3. d
4. b
5. d
6. T
7. F
8. T
9. T
10. T

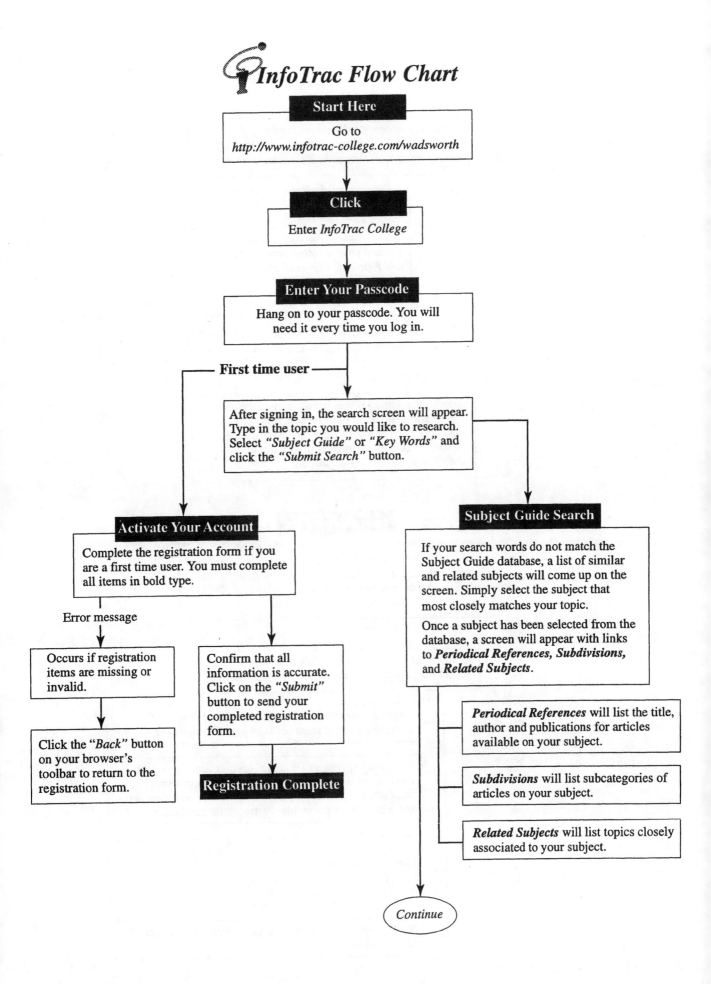

InfoTrac Flow Chart

Start Here

Go to
http://www.infotrac-college.com/wadsworth

Click

Enter *InfoTrac College*

Enter Your Passcode

Hang on to your passcode. You will
need it every time you log in.

First time user

After signing in, the search screen will appear.
Type in the topic you would like to research.
Select *"Subject Guide"* or *"Key Words"* and
click the *"Submit Search"* button.

Activate Your Account

Complete the registration form if you
are a first time user. You must complete
all items in bold type.

Error message

Occurs if registration
items are missing or
invalid.

Click the *"Back"* button
on your browser's
toolbar to return to the
registration form.

Confirm that all
information is accurate.
Click on the *"Submit"*
button to send your
completed registration
form.

Registration Complete

Subject Guide Search

If your search words do not match the
Subject Guide database, a list of similar
and related subjects will come up on the
screen. Simply select the subject that
most closely matches your topic.

Once a subject has been selected from the
database, a screen will appear with links
to *Periodical References, Subdivisions,*
and *Related Subjects*.

Periodical References will list the title,
author and publications for articles
available on your subject.

Subdivisions will list subcategories of
articles on your subject.

Related Subjects will list topics closely
associated to your subject.

Continue

Continue
Subject Guide
Search

A list will appear on the screen containing bibliographic information for each article in your search up to a maximum of 20 articles per page.

To select an article check the *"Mark"* box by clicking on it with your mouse.

To read your selected articles click on the *"View Text and Retrieval Choices"* link.

To narrow your search click on the *"Limit Search"* link located at the top of the list of articles screen.

The screen will narrow the search to reference articles with the full text available, by date, journal or word(s).

Your marked articles will have the bibliographic information at the top of the article followed by an abstract (when available) and the full text of the article. To browse through your articles, click on the *"Previous"* or *"Next"* button.

Using PowerTrac

With **PowerTrac**, a more complex search can be conducted. Click on the *"Down Arrow"* on the *"Select an Index"* listbox, choose the criteria you want to use. The code for your criteria will appear in the entry box. Type your criteria in the entry box after the code.

If you want to search by multiple criterion, simply repeat the process with an operator between them.

Logical operators (and/or/not) specify inclusive or exclusive relationships between search terms or result sets.

Proximity operators (Wn, Nn) specify that two search terms must be within a specified distance (in words) of each other. Proximity operators work only with free text indexes such as keywords, abstracts, text and titles.

Range operators (since, before, etc.) specify upper bounds, lower bounds or both in searches for numeric data. Numeric indexes include publication dates, number of employees and annual sales.

Nesting operators determine the order in which operators are evaluated.

PART 9

INFOTRAC KEY WORDS for
Issues and Ethics in the Helping
Professions, Sixth Edition

INFOTRAC COLLEGE EDITION RESOURCES
For additional readings, explore InfoTrac College Edition, our online library. Go to
http://infotrac.thomsonlearning.com/and select the key word searches given below. Key words are listed in a
form that enables the search engine to locate a wider range of articles in the online university library. Key words
should be entered exactly as shown, to include asterisks, "w1," "w2," "AND," and other search engine tools.

Chapter 1: Introduction to Professional Ethics
ethical decision making model*
ethical community standard*
standard* practice psych*
aspirational ethic*
mandatory ethic*

Chapter 2: The Counselor as a Person and as a Professional
countertransference
transference
counselor stress
counselor impairment
therap* impairment
mental AND health AND burnout

Chapter 3: Values and the Helping Relationship
Therap* values
values psych*
spiritual values in psych*
religious values in psych*
end of life decision*
rational suicide

Chapter 4: Multicultural Perspectives and Diversity Issues
ethic*
multicult*
values couns*
values therap*
values psych*
multicult training couns*
multicultural counseling competencies

Chapter 5: Client Rights and Counselor Responsibilities
informed w1 consent
informed consent couns*
informed consent therap*
record* couns*
record* therap*
mental health managed care
malpractice liability in psychotherapy
malpractice AND psych*
involuntary commitment
repressed w1 memory w1 syndrome
false memory

105

Chapter 6: Confidentiality: Ethical and Legal Issues
confidentiality psych*
privileged w1 communication
privacy couns*
privacy psych*
limits w2 confidentiality
duty to warn (17)
duty to protect (20)
suicid* client*
suicid* therap*
suicide w1 prevention
child abuse
confid* HIV
confid* AIDS

Chapter 7: Managing Boundaries and Multiple Relationships
dual relationship* couns*
dual relationship* psych*
multiple relationships
barter* psych*
barter* couns*
gift psych*
gift therap*
social w1 realtionship*client*
social w1 realtionship*therap*
sexual w1 attraction client*
sexual w1 relationship client*
touching psych*

Chapter 8: Professional Competence and Training
psychotherapist competence
training therap*
continuing education for mental health workers
education mental health
education psych*
training AND psychotherapy AND research
techniques in couns*
professional AND licensing AND mental health
professional AND licensing AND couns*
professional AND licensing AND psych*
credentialing mental health

Chapter 9: Issues in Supervision and Consultation
clinical W1 supervision
ethic*clinical superv*
legal clinical superv*
clinical superv* role*
clinical superv* responsib*
clinical superv* competence
multicult* supervision
multiple roles AND relationships in superv*
ethic* AND consultation AND psych*

Chapter 10: Issues in Theory, Practice, and Research
psychodiagnosis
ethical issue* AND diagnosis
ethical issue* test* couns*

Chapter 11: Ethical Issues in Couples and Family Therapy
ethics* family therap*
couples counseling ethical issues
value* marriage therapy
gender sensitive AND therapy
confidentiality in marital and family therapy

Chapter 12: Ethical Issues in Group Work
training of group w1 leader*
supervision AND group w1 leader*
co-leadership in group work
confidentiality AND groups
values in group counseling

Chapter 13: Ethical Issues in Community Work
community w1 counseling
community w1 mental w1 health
mental w1 health paraprofessional*

PART 10

LIST OF PROFESSIONAL ORGANIZATIONS AND WEBSITE RESOURCES for
Issues and Ethics in the Helping Professions,
Sixth Edition

CASEBOOKS AS A SUPPLEMENT TO TEACHING ETHICS

In addition to becoming generally familiar with the ethics codes of the various professional organizations, you might find the following ethics casebooks of the professional organizations useful in preparing for your classes. These casebooks illustrate standards and apply them to specific situations. There are case vignettes, articles, and discussions of ways to interpret specific sections of the codes in practical ethical dilemmas. The casebooks you may want to order for your use are:

- For the American Counseling Association
ACA Ethical Standards Casebook (Fifth Edition)
Barbara Herlihy and Gerald Corey (1996)
     This casebook is designed to provide a foundation for analytic evaluation of the standards in applying these principles in work with diverse client populations. It contains illustrative vignettes that encourage discussion and distinguish ethical practice from questionable or unethical practice. Nineteen original case studies (written by various authors) clarify complex areas of ethical conduct.
Order from the American Counseling Association
          5999 Stevenson Avenue
          Alexandria, VA 22304
          1-800-347-6647

- •For the American Psychological Association
Ethics for Psychologists: A Commentary on the APA Ethics Code
Mathilda B. Canter, Bruce E. Bennett, Stanley E. Jones, and Thomas F. Nagy (1994)
     This casebook is a practical resource to help students and practitioners learn and apply the APA Ethics Code. It deals with the ethical decision making process and provides commentaries to address questions that are likely to be raised by therapists with regard to a given standard. The last section puts the ethical principles in context by describing how psychology is regulated by professional organizations as well as by local, state, and federal laws.
Order from the American Psychological Association
          Book Order Department
          750 First Street, NE
          Washington, DC 20002-4242
          1-800-374-2721

- For the American Psychological Association
Ethics in Plain English: An Illustrative Casebook for Psychologists
Thomas F. Nagy (2000)
     This casebook is geared to the 102 standards of APA's Ethics Code, with illustrative fictional case vignettes. The aim of the book is to help readers take the ethical standards and apply them to a variety of situation.
Order from the American Psychological Association
          Book Order Department
          750 First Street, NE
          Washington, DC 20002-4242
          1-800-374-2721

- For the American Association for Marriage and Family Therapy

American Association for Marriage and Family Therapy Ethics Casebook (Second Edition)
Gregory W. Brock (Editor) (1998)
   This casebook contains specific case examples and discussions illustrating ethical practices regarding relationships with clients, supervisees, employees, third-party payers, and colleagues. It includes essays on dual relationships, confidentiality, impaired therapists, the role of clergy therapists, defensive supervision, and a U.S. survey of ethical behavior and attitudes of marriage and family therapists.
Order from the American Association for Marriage and Family Therapy
       1133 15th Street, NW, Suite 300
       Washington, DC 20005-2710
       (202) 452-0109

See also *Ethical Casebook for the Practice of Marriage and Family Counseling*, Patricia Stevens (Editor), published by the American Counseling Association.
Order from the American Counseling Association
       5999 Stevenson Avenue
       Alexandria, VA 22304
       1-800-347-6647

WEBSITE RESOURCES FOR ETHICS

American Counseling Association (ACA)
Student memberships are available to both undergraduate and graduate students enrolled at least half-time or more at the college level. ACA membership provides many benefits, including a subscription to the Journal of Counseling and Development and also a monthly newspaper entitled Counseling Today, eligibility for professional liability insurance programs, legal defense services, and professional development through workshops and conventions. ACA puts out a resource catalog that provides information on the various aspects of the counseling profession, as well as giving detail information about membership, journals, books, home-study programs, videotapes, audiotapes, and liability insurance. For further information, contact:
    American Counseling Association
    5999 Stevenson Avenue
    Alexandria, VA 22304 -3300
    Telephone: (703) 823-9800 or (800) 347-6647
    Fax: (703) 823-0252
    Website: http://www.counseling.org

American Psychological Association
The APA has a Student Affiliates category rather than student membership. Journals and subscriptions are extra. Each year in mid-August or late August the APA holds a national convention. Membership includes a monthly subscription to a journal, American Psychologist, and a magazine, Monitor on Psychology, 11 times a year. For further information contact:
    American Psychological Association
    750 First Street, N. E.
    Washington, DC 20002-4242
    Telephone: (202) 336-5500 or (800) 374-2721
    Fax: (202) 336-5568
    Website: http://www.apa.org

National Association of Social Workers (NASW)
NASW membership is open to all professional social workers and there is a student membership category. The NASW Press, which produces Social Work and the NASW News as membership benefits, is a major service in professional development. NASW has a number of pamphlets that are available. For information contact:
 National Association of Social Workers
 750 First Street, N. E., Suite 700
 Washington, DC 20002-4241
 Telephone: (202) 408-8600 or (800) 638-8799
 FAX (202) 336-8311
 Website: http://www.socialworkers.org

American Association for Marriage and Family Therapy (AAMFT)
The AAMFT has a student membership category. Members receive the Journal of Marital and Family Therapy, which is published four times a year, and a subscription to six issues yearly of Family Therapy News. For membership applications and further information contact:
 American Association for Marriage and Family Therapy
 1133 15th Street, N. W., Suite 300
 Washington, DC 20005-2710
 Telephone: (202) 452-0109
 Fax: (202) 223-2329
 Website: http://www.aamft.org

National Organization for Human Service Education (NOHSE)
The National Organization for Human Service Education's (NOHSE) is made up of members from diverse disciplines -- mental health, child care, social services, gerontology, recreation, corrections, and developmental disabilities. Membership is open to human-service educators, students, fieldwork supervisors, and direct-care professionals. Student membership is $28per year, which includes a subscription to the newsletter (the Link), the yearly journal, Human Services Education; and discount price for the yearly conference (held in October). For further information about membership in the National Organization for Human Service Education, contact:
 Chrisanne Christensen
 Sul Ross State University
 Rio Grande College
 Rt. 3 Box 1200
 Eagle Pass, TX 78852
 Telephone: (830) 758-5112
 Fax: (830) 758-5001
 Email: reddoc@altavista.net
 Website: http://www.nohse.com

PART 11

STUDENT EVALUATION OF THE COURSE AND THE INSTRUCTOR
for Issues and Ethics in the Helping Professions, Sixth Edition

Student Evaluation of the Instructor

Read each statement below that describes some facet of the instructor. Decide the degree to which you agree or disagree with each of the following statements about the instructor of this course. Use the following code:

5 = I strongly agree with this statement.
4 = I agree, in most respects, with this statement.
3 = I am undecided in my opinion about this statement.
2 = I disagree, in most respects, with this statement.
1 = I strongly disagree with this statement.

THE INSTRUCTOR OF THIS COURSE:
_____ 1. demonstrates a broad and accurate knowledge of most of the subjects in this course.
_____ 2. clearly presents the subject matter.
_____ 3. effectively adjusts to my level of comprehension.
_____ 4. enjoys teaching and has a high degree of enthusiasm.
_____ 5. welcomes differences of opinions.
_____ 6. demonstrates a respectful attitude toward students.
_____ 7. stimulates the intellectual curiosity of the students.
_____ 8. uses appropriate and useful teaching methods.
_____ 9. demonstrates an understanding and accepting attitude toward students.
_____ 10. provides an encouraging and supportive climate in the classroom.
_____ 11. invites students to seek personal help as a way of getting the most from the course.
_____ 12. clearly presents the objectives of the course.
_____ 13. is well-organized and utilizes class time effectively.
_____ 14. gives relevant and helpful out-of-class assignments.
_____ 15. is clear about the criteria for grading.
_____ 16. demonstrates fairness in determining grades.
_____ 17. creates a classroom atmosphere that is extremely helpful to learning.
_____ 18. addresses students concerns and seems genuinely interested in students progress in this course.
_____ 19. is friendly both in and out of class.
_____ 20. consistently abides by the policies and procedures as described in the course outline.

Evaluation of Course and Instructor

Please put in the blank the letter of the statement which you believe to be most true of this course or this instructor for each topic.

_____ 1. To what degree do you feel the objectives of this course were met?
a.   All of the important goals were met.
b.   Many of the goals were attained.
c.   Some of the goals were attained.
d.   Many of the goals were not attained.
e.   The important goals were not attained.

_____ 2. How much actual work and study outside of class did you do for this course?
a.   Much more than for most of my courses.
b.   More than for my other courses.
c.   About the same as for my other courses.
d.   Less than for most of my courses.

____ 3. How valuable was the textbook to you?
a. Outstanding in value.
b. Almost all parts were valuable.
c. Generally valuable.
d. Some parts worth reading.
e. A waste of time.

____ 4. How does the instructor of this course compare with instructors in other college courses you have taken?
a. One of the best.
b. Better than most.
c. About the same as most.
d. Worse than most.
e. One of the worst.

____ 5. This course has been:
a. extremely challenging.
b. very challenging.
c. somewhat challenging.
d. not too challenging.
e. extremely unchallenging.

____ 6. Compared with other classes, this class has been:
a. much more interesting.
b. more interesting.
c. about as interesting.
d. less interesting.
e. much less interesting.

____ 7. As far as learning material that will be of practical use in my college career and my life, this course has been:
a. very helpful
b. somewhat helpful.
c. not too helpful.

____ 8. Would you recommend this course, in terms of its content, to a good friend whose interests are like yours?
a. Yes, recommend it highly.
b. Yes, it is better than most courses.
c. Undecided.
d. No, it is not as good as most courses.

____ 9. Would you recommend this instructor to a good friend?
a. Yes, recommend the instructor highly.
b. Yes, the instructor is better than most.
c. Undecided.
d. No, the instructor is not as good as most.

____ 10. What overall rating would you give to this instructor?
a. Superior.
b. Very good.
c. Good.
d. Fair.
e. Poor.

_____ 11. What overall rating would you give to this course?
a. Superior.
b. Very good.
c. Good.
d. Fair.
e. Poor.

_____ 12. How would you assess the value of what you have learned from this course?
a. Learned or gained a great deal from this class.
b. Learned or gained enough from this class to make it worth the time.
c. Learned or gained little from this class.
d. Learned or gained almost nothing from this class.

For the following questions, please write a brief statement that reflects your honest view.

13. What topics in this course did you find most meaningful and of most value to you personally?

14. What topics in this course did you find least meaningful?

15. What other topic(s) would you like to see included in this course?

16. Which of your personal or academic concerns were not adequately addressed in this course?

17. Which assignments stand out as being most valuable to you?

18. To what degree has this course been useful in giving you ideas and tools that you can apply to all of your other courses?

19. To what degree did you read, study, and reflect on the material in the textbook?

20. Please make any other comments you wish or list any other suggestions for improving the course. And thank you for taking the time to complete this evaluation in an honest manner.

PART 12

OTHER BOOKS BY THE AUTHORS for
Issues and Ethics in the Helping Professions,
Sixth Edition

Here is a list of other books that my colleagues and I have authored or co-authored, and some educational student videos as well, that might be of interest to you. These books and videos are published by the Brooks-Cole / W a d s w o r t h   P u b l i s h i n g   C o m p a n y,   P a c i f i c   G r o v e,   C A 9 3 9 5 0 .

Corey, M. S., & Corey, G. (2003). *Becoming a Helper,* 4th ed.
Deals with topics of concern to students studying in one of the helping professions. Some of the issues explored are examining your motivations and needs, becoming aware of the impact of your values on the counseling process, learning to cope with stress, dealing with burnout, exploring developmental turning points in your life, and ethical issues.

Corey, G., Corey, M. S., & Callanan, P. (2003). *Issues and Ethics in the Helping Professions,* 6th ed.
A combination textbook and student manual that contains self-inventories, open-ended cases and problem situations, exercises, suggested activities, and a variety of ethical, professional, and legal issues facing practitioners.

Corey, G., Corey, M. S., & Haynes, R. (2003). *Ethics in Action: CD-ROM.*
This self-study program is aimed at exploring ethical decision making, the role of values in the counseling process, and managing boundary issues and multiple relationships. This CD-ROM contains video role-play segments along with exercises for interactive learning and can be used along with either *Becoming a Helper* or *Issues and Ethics in the Helping Professions.*

Corey, M. S., & Corey, G. (2002). *Groups: Process and Practice,* 6th ed.
Outlines the basic issues and concepts of group process throughout the life history of a group. Applies these basic concepts to groups for children, adolescents, adults, and the elderly.

Corey, G., & Corey, M. S. (2002). *I Never Knew I Had a Choice,* 7th ed.
A self-help book for personal growth that deals with topics such as the struggle to achieve autonomy; the roles that work, sex roles, sexuality, love, intimacy, and solitude play in our lives; the meaning of loneliness, death, and loss; and how we choose values and find meaning in life.

Corey, G. (2001). *The Art of Integrative Counseling.*
This brief supplementary book is an expansion of Chapter 14 in *Theory and Practice of Counseling and Psychotherapy.*

Corey, G. (2001). *Student Video and Workbook for the Art of Integrative Counseling.*
This 2-hour video brings theory into action as it is applied to the case of Ruth. Showing my own integrative style in counseling Ruth, I draw on the thinking, feeling, and behaving perspectives, highlighting the value of working with a singular theme from all three modalities of human experience.

Corey, G. (2001). *Case Approach to Counseling and Psychotherapy,* 5th ed.
Demonstrates how theory can be applied to specific cases using the theories that correspond to chapters in *Theory and Practice of Counseling and Psychotherapy.* Readers are challenged to apply their knowledge of these theories to the case of Ruth. Also, a proponent of each theory writes about his or her assessment of Ruth and demonstrates his or her particular therapeutic style in counseling Ruth. I then show how I might intervene with Ruth by staying within the general framework of each of these theories, and also in an eclectic, integrated fashion.

Corey, G. (2001). *Theory and Practice of Counseling and Psychotherapy,* 6th ed.
Presents an overview of 10 contemporary theories of counseling, with an emphasis on the practical applications and the therapeutic process associated with each orientation.

Corey, G. (2000). *Theory and Practice of Group Counseling,* 5th ed. (and *Student Manual,* 5th ed.).
A comprehensive group counseling textbook that describes 10 contemporary theories of group counseling and highlights techniques applicable to therapeutic groups.

Corey, G., Corey, M. S., & Haynes, R. (2000). *Evolution of a Group Video: Student Video and Workbook.*
This 2-hour self-study video/workbook package demonstrates group process in action and illustrates techniques for all the stages of a group. This video is also designed to be used in conjunction with *Theory and Practice of Group Counseling, Groups: Process and Practice,* and *Group Techniques.*

Corey, G., Corey, C., & Corey, H. (1997). *Living and Learning.* (Belmont, CA: Wadsworth).
Presents learning as a lifelong journey. By encouraging readers to use the world as their classroom and to "learn from living," this book helps readers to get more out of their college experience and the rest of their lives.

Corey, G., Corey, M. S., Callanan, P., & Russell, J. M. (1992). *Group Techniques,* 2nd ed.
Describes ideas for creating and implementing techniques for use in groups. Gives a rationale for the use of techniques in all the stages in a group's development.

For a copy of the latest Brooks-Cole / W a d s w o r t h   H u m a n   S e r v i c e s,
C o u n s e l i n g,   a n d   S o c i a l   W o r k   C a t a l o g,   c o n t a c t:

Brooks-Cole / W a d s w o r t h   P u b l i s h i n g   C o m p a n y
Source Code 8BCCNM01
511 Forest Lodge Road
Pacific Grove, CA 93950-5098
Phone: (800) 423-0563
Fax: (408) 375-6414
E-mail: *info@brookscole.com*
Website: *http://www.brookscole.com*

PART 13
TRANSPARENCY MASTERS for
Issues and Ethics in the Helping Professions,
Sixth Edition
by Mary Lou O'Phelan, *Century College*
Revisions by: John Perry

CONTENTS

Issues and Ethics
in the Helping Professions
6th Edition

by Gerald Corey, Marianne Schneider Corey, & Patrick Callanan

Wadsworth Group

A division of

Thomson Learning, Inc.

Ethical Decision Making: Key Terms

- Values
- Morality
- Law
- Community Standards
- Mandatory Ethics
- Virtue Ethics
- Professionalism

- Ethics
- Ethical Conduct
- Ethics
- Aspirational Ethics
- Principle Ethics
- Standards of Practice

Definitions: Key Terms

- **Law**
  - defines the minimum standards society will tolerate and is enforced by government

- **Ethics**
  - represents the ideal standards set and is enforced by professional associations

- **Aspirational Ethics**
  - refer to the highest professional standards of conduct to which counselors can aspire

- **Principle Ethics**
  - focuses on moral issues with the goal of solving a particular dilemma

- **Virtue Ethics**
  - focuses on character traits of the counselor and non-obligatory ideals

Basic Moral Principles to Guide Decision Making

- ❧ Autonomy
- ❧ Beneficence
- ❧ Nonmaleficence
- ❧ Justice
- ❧ Fidelity
- ❧ Veracity

Steps in Making Ethical Decisions

❧ The authors' approach to thinking through ethical dilemmas:

1. Identify the problem or dilemma

2. Identify the potential issues involved

3. Review the relevant ethics codes

4. Know the applicable laws and regulations

5. Obtain consultation

6. Consider possible and probable courses of action

7. Enumerate the consequences of various decisions

8. Decide on what appears to be the best course of action

Social Constructivism Model of Ethical Decision Making

❧ Redefines ethical decision making process as an interactive one

❧ This model involves negotiating when there is disagreement

❧ If consensus is not possible, further negotiating and interactive reflection need to occur

The Counselor as a Person and as a Professional

- Counselors must be aware of the influence of their own personality and needs

- Personal needs of counselors based on unresolved personal conflicts:

  - a need to tell people what to do

  - a desire to take away all pain from clients

  - a need to have all the answers and to be perfect

  - a need to be recognized and appreciated

  - a tendency to assume too much responsibility for the changes of clients

  - a fear of doing harm, however inadvertently

Issues and Ethics - Chapter 2 (1)

Transference

❧ Transference is the process whereby clients project onto their therapists past feelings or attitudes they had toward significant people in their lives

❧ Transference: the "unreal" relationship in therapy

• Counselors need to be aware of their personal reactions to a client's transference

• All reactions of clients to a therapist are not to be considered as transference

• Ethical issue is dealing appropriately with transference

Countertransference

❧ Countertransference is the counselor's reaction to the client's transference response

❧ Examples:

  ❧ being overprotective with a client

  ❧ treating clients in benign ways

  ❧ rejecting a client

  ❧ needing constant reinforcement and approval

  ❧ seeing yourself in your clients

  ❧ developing sexual or romantic feelings for a client

  ❧ giving advice compulsively

  ❧ desiring a social relationship with clients

Stress in the Counseling Profession

❧ Counseling can be a hazardous profession

❧ Some sources of stress for counselors are:

   ❧ Feeling they are not helping their clients

   ❧ The tendency to accept full responsibility for clients' progress

   ❧ Feeling a pressure to quickly solve the problems of clients

   ❧ Having extremely high personal goals and perfectionistic strivings

Counselor Impairment

- Impaired counselors have lost the ability to resolve stressful events and are not able to function professionally

- Shared characteristics of impaired counselors:

  - fragile self-esteem

  - difficulty establishing intimacy in one's personal life

  - professional isolation

  - a need to rescue clients

  - a need for reassurance about one's attractiveness

  - substance abuse

Maintaining Vitality as a Counselor

- Counselors are often not prepared to maintain their vitality

- Sustaining the personal self is an ethical obligation

- Personal vitality is a prerequisite to functioning in a professional role

- Main challenge is to create a balanced life in these areas:
  - Spirituality
  - Self-direction
  - Work and leisure
  - Friendship
  - Love

Values and the Helping Relationship

❧ Value conflicts:

- ❧ To refer or not to refer

- ❧ Referrals appropriate when moral, religious, or political values are centrally involved in a client's presenting problems and when:

  - ✦ therapist's boundaries of competence have been reached
  - ✦ therapist has extreme discomfort with a client's values
  - ✦ therapist is unable to maintain objectivity
  - ✦ therapist has grave concerns about imposing his or her values on the client

Values

❧ Development of value systems are influenced by:

- ✿ Family
- ✿ Peer group
- ✿ Culture
- ✿ Media
- ✿ Religion
- ✿ Education
- ✿ Politics

Value Areas

❧ **Education/New Knowledge**

❧ **Money/Possessions**

❧ **Religion/Morals**

❧ **Helping Others**

❧ **Friendships**

❧ **Work/Career**

❧ **Health—Emotional and Physical**

❧ **Love/Affection**

❧ **Achievement/Recognition**

❧ **Marriage/Family**

❧ **Security**

❧ **Leisure**

Role of Spiritual and Religious Values in Counseling

❧ Spirituality refers to:

  ❧ general sensitivity to moral, ethical, humanitarian, and existential issues without reference to any particular religious doctrine

❧ Religion refers to:

  ❧ the way people express their devotion to a deity or an ultimate reality

❧ Key issues:

  ❧ Can the counselor understand the religious beliefs of the client?

  ❧ Can the counselor work within the framework of the client?

Policy on End-of-Life Decisions

❧ Various continuing care or treatment options exist, such as:

   ❧ aggressive treatment of the medical condition(s)

   ❧ life-sustaining treatment

   ❧ medical intervention intended to alleviate suffering (but not to cure)

   ❧ withdrawing life-sustaining treatment

   ❧ voluntary active euthanasia

   ❧ physician-assisted suicide

Values Pertaining to Sexuality

❦ Counselors need to know their attitude toward:

&❧ the belief that sex should be reserved for marriage only

&❧ sex as an expression of love and commitment

&❧ casual sex

&❧ group sex

&❧ extramarital sex

&❧ premarital sex

&❧ homosexuality

&❧ teenage sex

Need for Multicultural Emphasis

❧ Key Terms:

- ❧ Ethnicity

- ❧ Minority group

- ❧ Multiculturalism (cross-cultural, transcultural, intercultural, similar meanings)

- ❧ Multicultural counseling

- ❧ Diversity-sensitive counseling

- ❧ Racism

- ❧ Stereotypes

- ❧ Culturally encapsulated counselor

Multicultural Competence

❧ **Recognizing our limitations**

❧ **Manifested in our willingness to:**

&❧ seek consultation

&❧ seek continuing education

&❧ make referrals

Counselor Attitudes in Working with Culturally Diverse Clients

❧ **Overt racist**

- overtly hostile, homophobic, racist, ageist, sexist, judgmental (should stay out of the field)

❧ **Covert prejudice**

- tries to hide negative, stereotyped opinions but client picks up cues

❧ **Culturally ignorant**

- lack of knowledge based on homogeneous background (need to learn about other cultures before working with them)

Counselor Attitudes in Working with Culturally Diverse Clients

❧ Color blind

 ❧ denies differences: "I don't recognize differences; I treat everyone the same."

❧ Culturally liberated

 ❧ recognize, appreciate, and celebrate cultural differences; strives for freedom from judgments of diverse clients

Examining Common Assumptions

❧ Assumptions about self-disclosure

❧ About assertiveness

❧ About self-actualization and trusting relationships

❧ About nonverbal behavior

❧ About directness

Cultural Issues in Counseling

❧ **Counselors will encounter diversity in areas such as:**

❧

- ❧ **gender**

- ❧ **race**

- ❧ **culture**

- ❧ **socioeconomic background**

- ❧ **physical ability**

- ❧ **age**

- ❧ **sexual orientation**

Cultural Issues in Counseling

❧ In dealing with diversity, counselors need to:

- acquire academic and experiential multicultural training

- develop working therapeutic relationships

- be flexible in applying theories

- be open to being challenged and tested

- be aware of their own value systems, potential stereotyping, and any traces of prejudice

Guidelines for Addressing Sexual Orientation

❧ In order to change therapeutic strategies, one must be open to changing assumptions about sexual orientation

❧ Counselors need to become conscious of their own faulty assumptions

❧ Counselors are challenged to confront their personal fears, myths, and stereotypes regarding sexual orientation

Counseling Gays and Lesbians

❧ **Exemplary practice includes:**

- ❧ not attempting to change sexual orientation without evidence that client desires change

- ❧ recognizing that gay and lesbian individuals can live happy and fulfilled lives

- ❧ recognizing the importance of educating others about gay and lesbian issues

- ❧ recognizing ways in which social prejudices and discrimination create problems for clients

Gay and Lesbian Myths

- Gay people can be identified by their mannerisms or physical characteristics

- Most gay people could be cured by having a good sexual experience with a member of the opposite sex

- The majority of child molesters are gay

- Gay people have made a conscious decision to be gay

- Gay adults will try to convert youth to their lifestyle

- Homosexuality is a psychological disorder that can be cured by appropriate psychotherapy

- In gay relationships, one partner usually plays the "husband/butch" role and the other plays the "wife/femme" role

- Homosexuality is caused by a defective gene

- Homosexuality is unnatural, since it does not exist in other species

Asian Americans

- ❦ I. Family structure patterns:

  - ❧ traditional gender roles

  - ❧ honor parents, listen to words of wisdom that come with age

  - ❧ extended family rules—especially within the first few generations

Asian Americans

II. Values and attitudes:

- education is the ladder to success

- persevere, don't give up

- self-denial is the secret to success

- respect traditions and culture of forefathers

- don't be ostentatious, forward, brash

- austerity and renunciation valued

- duty to family and country

- spiritual evolution sought

Checklist for Informed Consent

- Voluntary participation
- Client involvement
- Counselor involvement
- No guarantees
- Risks associated with counseling
- Confidentiality and privilege
- Exceptions to confidentiality and privilege
- Counseling approach or theory
- Counseling and financial records
- Ethical guidelines

Checklist for Informed Consent

- ❧ Licensing regulations
- ❧ Credentials
- ❧ Fees and charges
- ❧ Insurance reimbursement
- ❧ Responsibility for payment
- ❧ Disputes and complaints
- ❧ Cancellation policy
- ❧ Affiliation membership
- ❧ Supervisory relationship
- ❧ Colleague consultation

Content of Informed Consent

- The therapeutic process
- Background of therapist
- Costs involved in therapy
- The length of therapy and termination
- Consultation with colleagues
- Interruptions in therapy
- Clients' right of access to their files
- Rights pertaining to diagnostic labeling
- The nature and purpose of confidentiality
- Benefits and risks of treatment
- Alternatives to traditional therapy
- Tape-recording or videotaping sessions

Ethical Issues in Online Counseling

❧ It is the counselor's responsibility to examine the ethical, legal, and clinical issues related to online counseling

❧ Providing counseling services online is controversial

❧ There are potential legal issues that must be addressed, a few of which include:

   ☙ Competence of practitioner in providing online counseling

   ☙ Informing client of limits and expectations of the relationship

   ☙ Developing a plan for how emergencies can be addressed

Some Advantages of Online Counseling

❧ Reaching clients who may not participate in face-to-face therapy

❧ Improving client access in rural areas

❧ Increasing flexibility in scheduling

❧ Facilitating assigning and completing of client homework

❧ Augmenting a problem-solving approach

❧ Improving an orientation to the counseling process

❧ Enhancing the provision of referral services

Some Disadvantages of Online Counseling

❧ Danger of making an inaccurate diagnosis

❧ Compromising of confidentiality and privacy

❧ Problems involved in being able to protect suicidal clients

❧ Difficulties in attending to clients who are in crisis situations

❧ Absence of traditional client-therapist relationship

❧ Inability to address a range of more complex psychological problems

❧ Inability to deal with interpersonal concerns in the therapy process

Reasons for Malpractice Suits

- Failure to obtain or document informed consent
- Client abandonment
- Marked departures from established therapeutic practices
- Practicing beyond the scope of competency
- Misdiagnosis
- Crisis intervention
- Repressed or false memory
- Unhealthy transference relationships
- Sexual abuse of client
- Failure to control a dangerous client
- Managed care and malpractice

Signs of Child Abuse

- ❧ Wary of physical contact with adults
- ❧ Apparent fear of parents or going home
- ❧ Inappropriate reaction to injury
- ❧ Lack of reaction to frightening events
- ❧ Apprehensive when other children cry
- ❧ Acting-out behavior to get attention
- ❧ Fearful, withdrawal behavior
- ❧ Short attention span or learning difficulties
- ❧ Regression into earlier stages of development
- ❧ Sudden change in behavior
- ❧ Fearful reaction to questions about injury

Key terms

❧ Confidentiality

❧ Privileged communication

❧ Privacy

Limits of Confidentiality

❧ When clerical assistants handle confidential information

❧ When counselor consults

❧ When counselor is being supervised

❧ When client has given consent

❧ When client poses danger to self or others

❧ When client discloses intention to commit a crime

❧ When counselor suspects abuse or neglect of a child or vulnerable adult

❧ When a court orders counselor to make records available

Duty to Protect Potential Victims

❧ Identify clients who are likely to do physical harm to third parties

❧ Protect third parties from clients judged potentially to be dangerous

❧ Treat those clients who are dangerous

Liability for Civil Damages When Practitioners Neglect Duty by:

❧ Failing to diagnose or predict dangerousness

❧ Failing to warn potential victims of violent behavior

❧ Failing to commit dangerous individuals

❧ Prematurely discharging dangerous clients from a hospital

Legal Precedents

- **Tarasoff Case**
  - duty to warn of harm to self or others
  - duty to protect
- **Bradley Case**
  - duty not to negligently release a dangerous client
- **Jablonski Case**
  - duty to commit a dangerous individual
- **Hedlund Case**
  - extends duty to warn to anyone who might be near the intended victim and who might also be in danger
- **Jaffee Case**
  - communications between licensed psychotherapists and their clients are privileged and therefore protected from forced disclosure in cases arising under federal law

Issues and Ethics - Chapter 6 (5)

Guidelines for Implementing Duty to Warn Requirements

- Get informed consent

- Plan ahead through consultation

- Develop contingency plans

- Obtain professional liability insurance

- Involve the client

- Obtain a detailed history

- Document in writing

- Implement procedures to warn

Issues and Ethics - Chapter 6 (6)

Guidelines for Assessing Suicidal Behavior

- ❧ Take direct verbal warnings seriously

- ❧ Pay attention to previous suicide attempts

- ❧ Identify clients suffering from depression

- ❧ Be alert for feelings of hopelessness and helplessness

- ❧ Monitor severe anxiety and panic attacks

- ❧ Determine whether individual has a plan

- ❧ Identify clients who have a history of severe alcohol or drug abuse

- ❧ Be alert to client behaviors (e.g. giving prized possessions away, finalizing business affairs, or revising wills)

- ❧ Determine history of psychiatric treatment

Ethical Guidelines for Disclosure of a Client's HIV Status

❧ Sufficient factual grounds for high risk of harm to third party

❧ Third party is at risk of death or substantial bodily harm

❧ Harm to the third party is not likely to be prevented unless counselor makes disclosure

❧ Third party cannot reasonably be expected to foresee or comprehend high risk of harm to self

Recommendations to Professionals Who Counsel HIV Clients

- All limits to confidentiality should be discussed with the client at the outset of treatment

- Therapists must be aware of state laws regarding their professional interactions with HIV-positive clients

- Therapists need to keep current with regard to relevant medical information

- Therapists need to know which sexual practices are safe

Dual and Multiple Relationships

❧ Identify measures aimed at minimizing the risks:

- ❧ set healthy boundaries from the outset

- ❧ secure informed consent of clients

- ❧ discuss both potential risks and benefits

- ❧ consult with other professionals to resolve any dilemmas

- ❧ seek supervision when needed

- ❧ document in clinical case notes

- ❧ examine your own motivations

- ❧ refer when necessary

Accepting Gifts

❧ Questions to consider in making a decision of whether or not to accept gifts from the client

❧ What is the monetary value of the gift?

❧ What are the clinical implications of accepting or rejecting the gift?

❧ When in the therapy process is the offering of a gift occurring?

❧ What are the therapist's motivations for accepting or rejecting a client's gift?

❧ What are the cultural implications of offering a gift?

Recommendations Prior to Establishing a Bartering Relationship

❧ Evaluate whether it puts you at risk of impaired professional judgment

❧ Determine the value of goods or services in a collaborative fashion

❧ Determine the appropriate length of time for arrangement

❧ Document the arrangement

❧ Consult with experienced colleagues or supervisors

Bartering

❧ Additional guidelines to clarify bartering arrangements

 ❧ Minimize unique financial arrangements

 ❧ If bartering is used, it is better to exchange goods rather than services

 ❧ Both therapist and client should have a written agreement for the compensation by bartering

Signs of Unhealthy Professional Boundaries

- **I. Intimacy distortions**
  - falling in love with client
  - parentification of client

- **II. Inadequate boundaries**
  - not noticing boundary invasion
  - over-responsible for client
  - over-involvement with client
  - over-identification with client
  - role confusion/reversal
  - inappropriate touch
  - being manipulated by client's unreasonable demands
  - responding to inappropriate personal questions
  - acting on sexual attraction

Issues and Ethics - Chapter 7 (5)

Types of Sexual Abuse in Psychotherapy

❧ **Sexual touch as therapy**

❧ **"Learning to love" as therapy**

❧ **Exploring sexual identity**

❧ **Becoming romantically involved**

❧ **Brief loss of control**

❧ **"Bonding" and other types of closeness**

Suggestions on How Therapists Can Deal with Sexual Attraction to Clients

☙ **Acknowledge the feelings**

☙ **Explore the reasons for attraction**

☙ **Never act on feelings**

☙ **Seek out experienced colleague or supervisor for consultation**

☙ **Seek personal counseling if necessary**

☙ **Monitor boundaries by setting clear limits**

☙ **If unable to resolve feelings, terminate the relationship and refer**

Issues and Ethics - Chapter 7 (7)

Continuum of Sexual Contact Between Counselor and Client

Psychological abuse

- The client is put in the position of becoming caretaker of counselor's needs.

Covert abuse

- The counselor intrudes into client's intimacy boundaries by sexual hugging, professional voyeurism, sexual gazes, over-attention to client's dress and appearance, or seductive behavior

Overt forms of sexual misconduct

- Counselor initiates or allows sexual remarks, passionate kissing, fondling, sexual intercourse, oral or anal sex, or sexual penetration with objects

Perspectives on Competence

❧ Professional codes of ethics on competence have common themes.

❧ Counselors practice only within the boundaries of competence, based on:

- ❧ education
- ❧ training
- ❧ supervised experience
- ❧ state and national professional credentials
- ❧ appropriate professional experience

Making Referrals

When

❧ counselors become aware that they do not have skills to offer client needed services

❧ Counselors' value system is in direct conflict with client behavior, which will hinder the relationship

How

❧ counselors must have thorough knowledge of the type and caliber of service available in the community

Who

❧ client must agree that problem exists and be willing to work with referral

Issues and Ethics - Chapter 8 (2)

Ethical Issues in Training Therapists

❧ **Training programs have an ethical responsibility to:**

- establish clear selection criteria

- provide exposure to major contemporary counseling theories

- teach students strengths and limitations of theories

- combine academic and personal learning

- screen candidates to protect public from incompetent practitioners

- teach range of skills to work with diverse clients

- provide training in ethics

Certification and Licensure

❧ Certification

- ❧ voluntary attempt by a group to promote professional identity

- ❧ attempts to verify qualifications

- ❧ sets minimum standards

- ❧ does not assure quality practice

❧ Licensure

- ❧ governs professional practice

- ❧ highlights uniqueness of an occupation

- ❧ restricts both use of title and practice of occupation

Rights of Supervisees

- Supervisory sessions free from distractions
- To be fully informed of supervisor's approach
- Confidentiality with regard to supervisee's disclosure
- Confidentiality with regard to clients except as mandated by law
- Continual access to records maintained during supervision
- To provide feedback to supervisors concerning supervision experience
- To seek consultation from other professional as necessary

Issues and Ethics - Chapter 9 (1)

Legal Aspects of Supervision

- **1. Informed consent**

- **2. Confidentiality and its limits**

- **3. Liability**

  - direct liability

  - vicarious liability

Multicultural Issues in Supervision

❧ Dimensions of a good multicultural model:

- ❧ pluralistic philosophy

- ❧ cultural knowledge

- ❧ consciousness raising

- ❧ experiential training

- ❧ contact with racial and ethnic minorities

- ❧ practicum or internship with culturally diverse populations

Multiple Roles and Relationships in the Supervisory Process

❧ Sexual intimacies during training:

  ❧ core issue is difference in power and status

❧ Providing counseling for trainees:

  ❧ dual relationship standard of ethical conduct should be used

Ethical and Professional Issues in Consultation

- ❧ **Ethical standards for consultants**
- ❧ **Value issues in consulting**
- ❧ **Competence in consultation**
- ❧ **Consultant training**
- ❧ **Relationship issues in consulting**
- ❧ **Rights of consultees**
- ❧ **Issues involving consulting groups**

Diagnosis as a Professional Issue

🕹 Key terms:

- 🔖 Medical diagnosis

- 🔖 Psychodiagnosis

- 🔖 Differential diagnosis

- 🔖 Diagnosis and statistical manual of mental disorders (DSM-IV)

Arguments for Psychodiagnosis

❧ No third-party reimbursement without acceptable diagnosis

❧ Difficult to formulate treatment plan without defining problem

❧ Provides team members with a common frame of reference

❧ Allows therapists to rule out medical conditions

❧ Used to assess whether clients pose danger to self or others

❧ Provides framework for research

Arguments Against Psychodiagnosis

❧ **Emphasis of DSM is on pathology**

❧ **Can minimize uniqueness of client**

❧ **Ignores natural capacities for self-healing**

❧ **Can lead people to accept self-fulfilling prophecies**

❧ **Assumption that distress in family is result of individual pathology**

❧ **Many therapists not competent to use DSM diagnosis appropriately**

Using Tests in Counseling

It is important for counselors to:

- be familiar with tests being used and taking tests themselves

- recognize limits of competence to use and interpret tests

- know the reasons why a particular test is being used

- make clients aware that tests are merely tools that can provide useful information

- give test results, not simply test scores

- be sensitive to the ways in which clients respond to test results

- assure clients that test results will not be used against them

- assure confidentiality unless consent is given

- know the limitations of tests being used

Critical Ethical Issues in Managed Care

❧ **Informed consent**

❧ **Confidentiality**

❧ **Abandonment**

❧ **Utilization review**

Financial Incentives Inherent in Managed Care Tempt Both Practitioner and Payor to:

❧ **Deny and limit access to long-term therapy**

❧ **Narrow the clients' choice of a therapist**

❧ **Disrupt the continuity of care**

❧ **Rely on less qualified providers to provide services**

❧ **Use less qualified providers to review care**

❧ **Breach client confidentiality by giving reviewers too much personal information about clients**

❧ **Base practices on a business ethic instead of a professional ethic**

Consent for Release of Confidential Information

Example:

I authorize the following disclosure of information:

1. Name of therapist that is to make the disclosure.

2. Name of person or organization to which the disclosure is to be made.

3. Purpose of disclosure.

4. Extent or nature of information to be disclosed:

_____

Signature of client _____

Date consent was signed _____

I understand that my records are protected under the federal and state confidentiality regulations and cannot be disclosed without my written consent.

Ethics and Research

❧ Issues involved:

- ❧ informed consent

- ❧ deception

- ❧ withholding treatment

- ❧ research with training and personal growth

- ❧ cultural diversity

Ethical Standards in Couples and Family Therapy

- Responsibility to clients

- Confidentiality

- Professional competence and integrity

- Responsibility to students, employees, and supervisees

- Responsibility to research participants

- Responsibility to the professions

- Fees

- Advertising

Issues and Ethics - Chapter 11 (1)

Training Issues in Couples and Family Therapy

❧ Personal Characteristics of Family Therapists

- self-knowledge is critical, especially family-of-origin issues

❧ Training, Supervision, and Clinical Experience

- didactic methods
- experiential methods

❧ Values in Couples and Family Therapy

- value system of therapist has crucial influence on formulation and definition of problems

Gender-Sensitive Couples and Family Therapy

- **Challenging traditional gender roles**
- **Gender roles and stereotypes**
- **Feminist perspective on family therapy:**
  - placing same demands for change on both women and men
  - valuing women's request for change
  - challenging traditional roles
  - valuing expression of emotion and nurturance in both partners
  - challenging patterns of male dominance and female subordination
  - questioning gender-specific rules
  - valuing women's work in the family

Confidentiality in Couples and Family Therapy

❧ **Exceptions to confidentiality:**

- ❧ when mandated by law

- ❧ when it is necessary to protect clients from harm to self or others

- ❧ when family therapist is a defendant in a civil, criminal, or disciplinary action arising from therapy

- ❧ when a waiver has been previously obtained in writing

Informed Consent in Couples and Family Therapy

Before therapy begins, the counselor needs to give information to family members about:

- purpose of therapy
- typical procedures
- risks of negative outcomes
- possible benefits of therapy
- the fee structure
- limits of confidentiality
- rights and responsibilities of clients
- the option that a family member can withdraw at any time
- what can be expected from the therapist

Ethical Issues in Group Therapy

❧ Professional training standards

- ❧ knowledge competencies
- ❧ skill competencies

❧ Training for various types of groups

- ❧ task and work groups
- ❧ psychoeducational groups
- ❧ group counseling
- ❧ group psychotherapy

Issues and Ethics - Chapter 12 (1)

Training Program for Group Workers

❧ **Recommendations**

  ❧ **personal psychotherapy**

  ❧ **self-exploration groups**

  ❧ **participation in a training and supervisory group**

Ethical Issues in Group Membership

- Informed consent
- Screening and selection
- Preparing group participants
- Involuntary participation
- Freedom to leave group
- Psychological risks
- Confidentiality in groups
  - exceptions to confidentiality
  - confidentiality with minors

Unethical Use of Group Techniques

❧ It is unethical for group leaders to use techniques:

&ra; that are unfamiliar

&ra; to serve a hidden agenda or enhance power

&ra; solely to create an intense atmosphere

&ra; to pressure members or deprive them of their dignity

Recommendations in Using Group Techniques

- Techniques should have therapeutic purpose

- Techniques should be grounded in a theoretical framework

- Client's self-exploration should be fostered

- Leaders should modify techniques for culturally diverse clients

- Techniques shouldn't be used haphazardly

- Techniques should be introduced in timely and sensitive manner

- Group members should be given freedom to participate or pass on experiment

- Group leaders should use techniques they are familiar with

- Leaders should be aware of potential impact of techniques

Four Facets of Comprehensive Community Counseling Programs

1. Direct community services

    ❧ preventive education

2. Indirect community service

    ❧ influencing policymakers

3. Direct client services

    ❧ focuses on outreach activities

4. Indirect client services

    ❧ client advocacy

Issues and Ethics - Chapter 13 (1)

Alternative Counselor Roles

- Change agent

- Consultant

- Adviser

- Advocate

Community Counseling Practitioner

Duties involve:

- Ability to support community needs

- Develop partnerships in creation and delivery of services

- Promote community organization and development of activities

- Outreach

- Develop strategies to empower the community

- Consultation with community agencies

- Evaluating human-services programs

- Advocate and assist with initiatives

- Develop and build community assets

Relationships Between Counselor and the Agency

- **Counselors who are dissatisfied with an agency or the system may decide to:**

  - subvert it any way they can

  - conform to institutional policies out of fear

  - make compromises between institutional demands and personal requirements

  - leave the agency

Case Management

❧ Philosophy

- 🐛 The primary goal of case management is to enable clients to achieve economic and personal independence and self-sufficiency

❧ The role of case manager

- 🐛 identify which needs and desires could motivate the client to change

- 🐛 help clients identify options and resources that can facilitate change and identify barriers blocking change

- 🐛 provide information options and resources that make change seem achievable

- 🐛 actively involve clients in all phases of the process